# In the Eye of Grief

# In the Eye of Grief

*Charlene Farrell*

PAPER TOWNS
PUBLISHERS

PAPER TOWNS
PUBLISHERS

First published by 2025

Papertowns Publishers
72, Vishwanath Dham Colony,
Niwaru Road, Jhotwara,
Jaipur, 302012

**In the Eye of Grief**



ISBN Print Book – 978-93-6185-176-6



Printed in India

# Dedication

This book is dedicated to none other than my wonderful dad, Clarence.

You will always have my love... in the eye of the storm and through it...

# Contents

# Preface

This book is a book of love and tribute. It came about during the toughest journey of my life. On the 17th of November 2024, I lost my wonderful dad. He was ailing for a year before he finally passed. I never thought I would feel such overwhelming loss in this lifetime, having always had an undeniably horrific and extreme fear of losing the people I love, also called Thanatophobia (the death anxiety). All through my life I have lived with this phobia, never intentionally giving it much attention, but having to deal with it every time my parents or other members of my family fell ill or had to go somewhere for extended periods of time.

That year, I battled this phobia so hard, and life just kept shoving it in my face. Dada was diagnosed with Liver Disease in February of 2024 and from then on, life has completely transformed for us all. From the battles of acceptance to the realisation that *this* was *it*, it took so much out of all of us who watched him leave this world. If only I'd had something to prepare me for what lay ahead, I think I would have held on tighter to every moment we still had left. There were times when I was so adamant to have him survive that I fought tooth and nail to have him receive the best care, when probably all he would have really wanted was for me to let him live out those days with experiences he wanted to enjoy for the "last time." Oh! The battles we had about food. Through this book I hope to ignite a tiny spark of realisation, a moment of calm, and hopefully a guidance of what to look for.

This book is inspired by the terrible loss of someone so seemingly permanent in life. When a parent dies, there is so much you are unprepared for: waking up with a hole in your chest and a void in the room; the simple things they did becoming reminders of how fleeting life is; how living without them changes the very core of who you are. The permanence of loss is what hit me the hardest, and I realised that preparation is totally underrated. There were those who kept telling me to prepare, and I just kept telling them it wasn't his time yet. I guess it was more me lying to myself about something plain to see.

Loss also brings with it multiple moments of realisation. It takes you on journeys you never thought you'd go on—from understanding how cherished you are in the eyes of those left behind, to the harsh reality of human nature and how it unravels. When you are going through the most difficult time of your life, you also see who really sticks around. Grief opens up a whole new reality to you.

Articulating grief was my first challenge, because everyone tries to define it in words. I realised through this journey that words don't do justice to an emotion like grief. It is complex; it rips you apart and, in some ways, puts you back together in a way you have never been put together before. There is something spiritual that shifts when you experience grief and, during this journey, I found the most solace in that. I wrote this little book in the hope it helps with that discovery too.

The journey is a long one, but it is also inevitable. Here, I have tried my best to keep this book as an experiential narrative rather than a guidebook. For one, I have learnt a lesson I am happy to have learnt: No two people will go through it the same way. I want this message out there loud and clear. There is no right or wrong way to grieve, and absolutely no definite steps to take. There are personal experiences that hit at various times from various places. Grief changes you—it re-moulds you. It hits you hard and then is gentle with you. But it is permanent, and it is raw.

I also hope to have this serve as a small guide to those around a griever. There have been so many times in the past year when the rage tried to break free and attack. This happened a lot because in the world we live in, very little is said about grief and what to expect and less still is shared about how to handle people who are grieving. We don't treat it with near enough importance as is required. There ought to be etiquette classes that include speaking to people suffering devastating loss. Sadly, even people who have been through grief don't think before they speak or act. The number of "I know how you feel" I've heard over the last few months has been shocking. The number of "But in *my* case it was like..." was annoying. There are people who have not lost parents who have walked up to me and said, "My parent is ill, so I know how you must be feeling," and this was the kicker. In some cases I have held my tongue so hard I found it difficult to breathe. In other cases, I let them know exactly what was on my mind. Let's just say, the number of "friends" I now have has quickly dwindled and that is okay. Loss is a journey that many will take and I hope some solace is found in these pages.

The book contains narrative and poetry. Poetry has always been my go-to mode when there was an emotional battle that I was trying to deal with. Dada loved my poetry and would always say he wanted me to publish a collection of it. All my life I have questioned if my poetry was worth putting together to publish. While writing this book, it never occurred to me once. All I want is for the most raw emotion to come out on paper. The battles of the heart can only be deciphered when it is in its truest, rawest most vulnerable form. If not all of it, I do hope some of it resonates.

This book is also dedicated to the ones who have held me up during this time: My mom, who suffered the loss the hardest—she lost her soulmate, her best friend, her companion. My sister, whose calm composure through the roughest storms in her life were tested beyond measure now. Dada passed away while she was away at work, the day before her birthday nonetheless. My niece, Maegan, who was her grandfather's princess—she meant the world to him and he meant the world to her. At such a young age, dealing with loss is difficult and she had to do it during a year of important examinations. Friends and family stayed close.

Finally, this book is a work of love and a tribute to the man who has made me who I am today. The man with a laugh that would warm a heart, a heart that would give more than it had, and a mind that worked from experience and passion. My Dada was my hero, my strength and my strongest supporter. This book is dedicated to his memory and written to help others deal with the brutality of grief. He always believed in helping others—that was the cornerstone of his life. Sometimes, watching him do what he did was exhausting. If I am to be even a smidgen of the person he was, I must share my experience if it would help even just one other person.

# CHAPTER 1

# An Introduction to the First Man I Ever Loved

It's been the most difficult period in my life. That day my world changed. I changed. Everything around me... changed. Every moment, every sensation, every sound has been etched into my memory like a message chiselled in stone. For all eternity I shall remember every sensation in my body and how that moment unfolded. It plays on in slow motion in my mind's eye—the way his skin felt to my touch, how every thought crossed my mind, and how he slowly, gently, almost poetically, slipped away from my grasp. One moment he was my Dada and the next, my guardian angel.

To start this narration, it is important first to know the person he was. Larger than life and opinionated to the extent that I would sit there biting my tongue even though I uttered not a word. He was the kind who always wanted to have a good time—the party would begin when he walked in the room. He was fun yet caring; loud but compassionate; opinionated yet sensitive. Such a conundrum was he. I don't think anyone ever truly knew who he was, and we are still learning about him from people—some of them strangers—whose lives he changed in ways we never expected.

A man with a smile who could light up the room
One who was calm when around there was doom
He helped those who had not a stitch on their shoulders
He cleared for the world the stones and the boulders
Where he went was laughter, fun and cheer,
Where he went was peace, safety, no fear.
My strength and my anchor is what he was
He taught me to stand for and fight for a cause.
The warmth that he exuded was for all to feel,
Never excluded, with everyone he'd deal.
My hero, without a cape he would soar,
A gentleman who would always hold open the door.
No man will ever hold a candle to him
He was everything, is everything, always... him

To know him was to know cheer. To know him was to know love and laughter. He was the very meaning of all those words—the epitome, so to speak. I have yet to meet people who thought otherwise. Their first words to describe him were *jovial, laughing, always cheerful*. Now I feel like a disgrace to his legacy, for I can't stop the tears that sneak out of the corner of my eyes ever so often. I was not prepared. Even though he gave me about a year—I was not prepared. I am still not prepared for every new day, for all around I feel the pain of him not being where he is meant to be. He was supposed to be here, supposed to do this, supposed to do that. Alas, never will he get down to it.

Never...

There's that word again—NEVER. A word that has plagued my mind all along. Never will I be able to argue with him again. Never will I get to eat a scrumptious steak prepared by him, just how I liked it, a secret only he knew. Never will I get to hold his hand again or to pose for a picture with his arm around my shoulder. Never will I hear the word "Charlu" ever again...

Never again didn't mean very much
Until you left, I didn't know.
Never again was never so final
Until you were gone for sure.

Such a loaded word these letters make
I never bothered to see,
Until *never* barged into my life,
Until it strangled me.

Five letters, they seem harmless at first,
But what we do not realise
Is that *never* may one day just be a word,
The next, the tears in our eyes.

Every time I sit now, my mind can think of nothing but my dad. We were quite the pair when I was a child, but we slowly drifted apart. Time and hormones made it impossible for us to see eye to eye on most things. In retrospect, that was probably because we were the same person—except I am female and he, male. We shared the same temperament and instincts in almost every situation. The clashes, however, came because we fought battles only we comprehended through lenses that only we could see through. When we were together and not clashing, nothing could get in the way—not even mom, who is still my backbone. When Dada and I were on the same page, heaven help the one who tried to come between us.

Anything was possible
With you by my side.
From you I never
Could possibly hide.

The safest spot of all
Was only with you.
My hero, you would make
Any dream come true.

My biggest cheerleader
Was you defined
You would get me out of
Every small bind.

Now I have a space,
Empty and bare
I am limbless and pointless
Without you there.

There was so much about him that made him unlike anyone I've ever met and yeah, I know every child feels that way about their dad. The tough part was getting to know him more *after* he left. People have come up to us during our period of grief to tell us how they knew him, leaving us in awe of the stories we were not privy to when he was around. Like the fact that he would keep a flask of tea outside for the car-washer at four in the morning, or he'd call the lady who weeded the garden in for tea and biscuits with him, or that he made donations to various causes that we never knew about.

Everyone had a different story to tell. The one that stays with me is what mom told me from when they were really young and had just started dating. They had gone to a Christmas dance. He was wearing a new suit he was very proud of. While he was walking mom back home, they came across a homeless person shivering in the December chill. Without a second thought, he pulled off his new suit jacket and wrapped it around the homeless man's shoulders, then walked away as though nothing had happened. That is the kind of *kind* I want to be—the quiet, unadvertised kind; kindness private and shared only between you and the other.

No task was too grand for you,
No help a mighty ask.
With a smile and a chuckle you'd do it
A small and a major task.

No distinction was made by you;
You cared not for what they wore.
It was the human, the living being,
For whom the weight you bore.

Be it a man by the side of the street
Or even a dog that starved,
There was not a being that would be ignored,
Whose problems you didn't want halved.

He was a proud man too, with opinions he researched in his own way, seldom open to change. He loved friendly arguments with those who tested his knowledge and I dare say, often won them.

We had a confusing relationship. His approval meant everything to me. I'd share a thought or an idea, hoping for a particular response. When that didn't come, my mood would cloud over, and no one could cheer me up. I loved him with every fibre of my being, but to say the relationship was volatile is an understatement. He'd say right, I would say left. If he said black, I'd say white. We were diverse in opinion but in truth, exactly the same.

When I looked in the mirror,
The similarities I'd not find.
When people told me I was like you.
I would think it very unkind.

I didn't like the comparison,
I wanted none to be true.
Why would they say it?
Why did I remind them of you?

But now that I've thought well about it,
And now that I'm seeing more clear,

I am everything like you
I am a picture of my father dear.

From the way I like things sorted
To the way I need things done;
To the fact that I don't like to be wrong,
To the fact that now life's undone.

We were and always will be
Reflections in the mirror true.
I am just what they said I was
The mirror reflection of you.

His love for life was infectious. He was always on the move. At work he was like a butterfly, fluttering around, knowing everything about everything and making sure the tiniest things were taken care of. He had an eye for detail that was sometimes exhausting. Everything had to be aesthetically pleasing and logically workable, which to me seemed like a senseless waste of time. He was the kind to rally behind his people, always willing to listen and speak up for the tiniest voice in the crowd.

As a lover of music, Englebert Humperdinck was practically family—his baritone woke us up every morning as kids. And oh! How Dada loved to perform his songs. Karaoke was his moment to shine. He'd stand there with one hand in his pocket and the other holding the mic, the trademark smirk on his face ready to wow the crowd with the first note. He got them every time. People would rush up to tell him how amazing his voice was, saying, "Now we know where Chrystal gets that voice from!" And oh, how he basked in all that glory—his grin, larger than life, his ability to get a crowd to its feet. That was dad.

I never told him how much I wanted to be like him—to have his ability to make everyone around him feel like the most important person in the room. I never told him that I watched how he worked a crowd and aspired to be able to be half the person he was.

His work ethic was unmatched—*work through it all* was his motto. As a hotelier, he noticed everything and everyone. As a child I'd often follow him around while he inspected the property once everyday. Every plant, every structure and every person had an important place. The gardeners were addressed by name, their families asked after. The plants had to be the perfect colour—if not, they weren't getting the love and care they deserved. The little statues and ornaments had to be well scrubbed until they gleamed.

He taught me how to eat, what cutlery was for what, and described cuisines in detail. He exposed us to every kind of food and experiences—from eating at the finest restaurants around the world to experiencing the smallest, most rustic eateries and dhabas in and around town. He taught us the importance of elegance in any and every surrounding and made sure we were appreciative of all who waited on us in any way.

There was so much about him that made him so special, so different, such an outstanding personality. Words don't do him justice. To truly know him, you had to meet him—even for a few hours. I had friends a quarter his age who would get completely taken up by his personality and wanted to spend time with him. He had a way of making people feel seen and heard.

There is definitely so much left unsaid to and about this man whose presence once felt so permanent. Most days I still expect to see him seated on his chair with his legs dangling off the arms. I wish I'd said more. I wish I had more time. I wish there were a few more moments. So many wishes but death brings a finality that leaves a gaping void.

And so, as I continue this narrative, you may identify with some of these experiences, or maybe not—because no two experiences are ever alike. Consider these pages as **another** perspective on death and dying—perhaps even a companion on your own journey with this one experience that we are all sure to have one day or the other.

# CHAPTER 2

# THE YEAR THAT WAS

Christmas of 2023 was unlike all others. We had such a fun time. It was the truest form of family time we had had in years. My sister is an entertainer and thus, Christmas and New Year's were the busiest, but this year, she was home for Christmas after years. Dada insisted we celebrate it with every ounce of gusto we could muster. The revelry didn't stop. However, even though we had the best time, I could make out he was much slower than usual and didn't seem to be as energetic. He was always the life of the party, but this Christmas he was a much more toned-down version. That was probably the first indication that something was not right.

When someone falls ill, you never believe that it is something that will take them from you. It was just another little bump in the road and, as a family, we would get through it. Or so we thought. In February of 2024, Dada was diagnosed with cirrhosis of the liver. This was a man who would be dragged for check ups every year by his ever-worried wife. He quit drinking immediately and never touched a drop of alcohol again. He never really drank that much, sometimes in the evenings or at a party. So when they said cirrhosis, we just couldn't understand it. Could it be the meds he was on? Or something we missed? Before this diagnosis, he had a heart attack in 2007. After that he was the poster child for health. Oh! But, he was diabetic for as long as I can remember too.

The beginning of the year was him slowing down. His feet would swell and that would make it difficult for him to walk. That was so difficult to watch, as Dada had always been the one we would find it difficult to catch up to. He was faster than all of us.

Watching you slow down
Was difficult for me;
Watching you struggle on a walk
Was not easy to see.

From the way you used to move about,
The dancing and the spring in your step,
To not getting up to dance anymore
And having to wait to catch your breath.

You were always so much more to me
Always on the move;
My hero without a cape,
My man with super groove.

The very words you'd speak to me
Were full of so much strength;
But then you spoke so slow, with a slur,
You spoke with your head bent.

The worst experiences we had began in March of 2024. It was a sudden day that was a shock to the system. One day he was his usual self; the next, a completely different person. It started with him confusing the TV remote for his phone and vice versa. It would irritate him that the television refused to switch on when he tried to put it on with his phone. And it would really agitate him when none of us could help.

There was this one day when we were sitting around, and mom came out of their room almost in tears, saying she couldn't understand what he wanted. I walked in thinking she was exaggerating, but that was not the case. He was sitting there, all confused, and kept telling me to change the channel, putting the phone in my hand. I tried to muster all the patience and understanding I could and explain to him that the phone was to take and make calls and send and receive messages, and the TV remote was to switch on the TV. He got really mad at me and insisted that we all knew nothing and were dumb and stupid. This was scary to me, as never once had he ever spoken to me that way. Instead of being patient, I lost it. I screamed and yelled back at him and this back-and-forth went on till I left the room.

For the life of me, I didn't understand what was going on. I just felt like he was being stubborn. We asked the doctors what this could be but their lack of response was quite frustrating. "It could be the beginning of dementia." That was the first diagnosis stated in passing. So then I began reading. Everything I could get my hands on about dementia, I devoured. I kept trying to find solutions and help. I scoured through tips on arresting the development of the condition, collected helpline numbers, and spoke to people who cared for loved ones with dementia. I just felt confused, helpless and oh so afraid. I read somewhere that this condition could take about ten years to progress from one stage to another, and that scared me even more. How could we do this for ten years? Now, I wish I did have those ten years. But alas, that's not what it was.

That vacant stare,
The eyes not seeing;
The confused mind,
Not knowing where you've been.

The fear kept increasing
With each passing day
How could we ever do this
When there was nothing there?

You had no idea
Of what was going on;
The anger came out
From dusk to dawn.

All night you would wander
From room to room aimlessly;
If only I could have helped
And saved you consciously.

The nights were the most difficult. We had to watch him closely and make sure he wouldn't wander out the door. My mother would keep awake most of the night and I'd check in every now and then. The fatigue was gripping. I worked during the day and played watchdog during the night.

One fine day, we decided to consult another doctor. That doctor said that the reason he was drifting to an altered reality was probably because his haemoglobin was too low. Now that seemed like an easy and quick fix. All we needed was to get him to a hospital and get iron infusions done—three infusions, once every week. And so the treatment began. Just after the first infusion was when I saw him slowly coming back. His restlessness was ebbing and he was becoming calmer and more patient. He was also less confused. By the last infusion, my dear Dada was back to his normal ways, walking around watering his plants all over again. Mom, my sister, and I were so relieved and ecstatic to have him back to normal. He carried on his medication and was quite hale and hearty.

Dada was back to his normal self and life as we had always known it was becoming a possibility again. Yes, he was still slow and his feet were still swelling, but mentally he was as sharp as a whip again. Every time we felt his mind remotely fade, we got him some iron-rich foods and he would generally come back to normal in a few hours.

Hope is a word,
Oh! so strong;
It makes things clearer,
Rights what's wrong.

It was that word,
That little feeling,
That got us through
It started the healing.

I can't express
The joy, the bliss,
At seeing you back,
So we wouldn't miss.

Hope is what got us
Through all of that pain;
It gave us a chance
To love and laugh again.

Hope—that is what this quick fix brought to us. A little confusion on his face, and beetroot and drumsticks were made for every meal. And so we trudged along, living life as usual.

One day in July, Dada fell ill with the flu. He had a runny nose that eventually led him to getting a fever. This fever kept rising. No matter how many paracetamols he had, it just wouldn't relent. We tried everything and then, finally, a friend came in with a traditional remedy. She rubbed a locally brewed cashew alcohol on the soles of his feet, on the top of his head, and on his belly. We never really believed in these remedies, but we were willing to try anything. Finally, the temperature began to settle. Another close call. We were very glad to have him out of that temperature and the delirium that accompanied it. I remember looking at him in bed, thinking, thank God he's okay.

There was always this, "Thank God, now we can help him and get him the treatment he needs" feeling that would accompany every bout of illness. The day after the entire episode, I came home from work to find mom very worked up. She was ranting about how stubborn Dada was, a rant I was very familiar with. This was a narrative that I'd heard all my life. "Such a stubborn man! He doesn't listen to anyone! He thinks he knows it all."

It took some calming and some patience to get to the bottom of this new rant. *What could have happened between the time I left for work and now?* I wondered. *Just yesterday there was so much love and concern in the room and now, exasperation.* Mom told me he was refusing to continue taking his medication. *What? How on earth did he arrive at that decision?* I thought in disbelief. The doctors were very clear that these meds were for life.

I asked Dada why he decided this. He said, with a smile, "Mama said I don't need them". Not my mama, his... She had been dead since 2014. That was it. No matter what we said he would not relent. He was happy not taking those pills and we were just hoping against hope that it would not have an adverse effect. As logic would have it, an adverse effect is exactly the kind of effect stopping his medication would have.

One day, while we were sitting around, I noticed his knees were very shiny and swollen. There we had it: the adverse effect. Even then mom kept begging him to take his meds, but he was adamant that the meds were not good for him. Apparently, his mom appeared to him in a dream and told him so. Who were we to refute that? A few days later, the swelling got so bad that he actually started oozing liquid from his body. And so, he had to spend the next five days in the hospital.

A mind so strong
A will that couldn't be shaken
A very positive attribute,
But at times it was mistaken.

Every day you would decide
What your day would be;
It was all your decision
How much help you'd need.

And to this day, I cannot believe
That you just had your say;
It was your plan, it was your mind
You only did it your way...

He hated being in the hospital, but he had no choice. The swelling had to be reduced and all the work that had been done was now undone because he had stopped taking his meds for about three weeks. This was the reset we could not afford with his health, and it proved to be the straw that broke the camel's back.

During this stint at the hospital is when we really started bonding again. He was so easy to deal with. He was calm and cool and basically looked after himself. He didn't need assistance to go to the washroom or anything else. All I was there for was company. We laughed at the nonsense playing on the tiny television they had up there. We joked about the way the guy who brought the food got so fond of him that he would sneak sugar into his tea, even though he was diabetic. In retrospect, I'm so glad he got to have that time and enjoy his tea. At that time, I wanted to physically harm that cafeteria guy.

His stint in the hospital ended five days later with him fit as a fiddle. Ready to take on the world, with a new list of medication and a promise that he would never again try such a silly stunt. No more missing medication, and for the months that followed, he stuck to his word. He would take those medicines regularly, but sadly the damage was already done.

He came home a happy camper,
Ready to take on the world.
All his days were structured well
All was calm until the months unfurled.

Oh! How I wish he didn't take
From his meds that irreversible break;
Never in our wildest dreams did we imagine
The toll on his life it would take.

Just a few weeks were all it took
To undo the repair that was done;
The repercussions of those few days
Could never be imagined by none.

Why, oh dad, why?
Could you just not do as asked
Maybe if you did just do that,
We wouldn't be speaking about you in the past.

He came home with all that suave he always had, pottering around the house again, watering his plants and doing small things here and there. I felt this sense of calm wash over me and kept telling myself, "It looks like everything is going to be alright." His feet were still swelling on and off, but other than that, things seemed normal. He was back to his normal self, arguing about what he couldn't eat and getting irritated as we were "depriving" him of his sweets.

There was a major internal rebellion that began brewing at this time. Dada loved his food and sweets. Do we indulge him and let him be happy, or do we curtail? At that time, curtailing was the only thing that would keep him safe and, therefore, unhappy. No sugar, not too much salt, no alcohol at all, not even a drop. He did not care about the alcohol anymore, but the sweets... oh man! The sweets. He wanted something sweet after his meals and some sweetness in his tea. And that was the cause of a lot of arguments.

I couldn't wrap my head around the fact that this grown man couldn't understand that he needed to watch what he ate. It was like dealing with a child. I didn't know how to get him to understand. Yes, there were times when I would lose my cool and be unable to deal with the stress. I'd get angry and shout at him, and he'd get angrier and shout back. Definitely nothing new. Even before he got ill, we were known for the battles we fought against each other. Neither of us backed down because we were just that good, and we each knew the right answer to everything.

Someone once asked me, "Are you going to prolong his life and watch him be angry, or are you going to give him the best damn years he's ever dreamed of?" Well, I was selfish. I admit it. I wanted to keep him with me for as long as I could. So I curtailed and curtailed and curtailed. Another reason to rip into each other, and so I chose to prolong his life and watch him get angry at me

September was quite uneventful other than the swelling of his feet. He went about doing what he normally loved, watering his plants and feeding biscuits to the dogs in the colony. His birthday was on the 26th of September. He loved that day and every year he'd get excited like a little boy. He would love it when we sang "Happy Birthday" and enjoyed cutting that cake. Every year we popped champagne at the stroke of midnight and he would bring out his best glasses for the celebration.

Like a little child
Excitement would appear
You were so excited,
For your birthday was here.

Popping the champagne
And singing the birthday song,
You loved the celebrations
All year long.

The last was unlike the others;
Your smile was not from the heart.
I didn't know then
That was the last—then we'd part

The final year, his birthday was not like it usually was. There was no smile on his usually ever smiling face. This year his glance was fleeting, his stare... vacant. That day, I knew he was dipping again. If only I could have seen it clearer, I'd have known this was the last time I could say the words "Happy Birthday Dada". If only I'd have known, I'd have wished him every hour. Alas, I didn't know. Since his birthday was mid-week, we celebrated it on the 21st instead. By the time his actual birthday came about, he had retreated again into a recess of his mind that none of us had access to. All day he sat in his room watching television. I wished him a happy birthday, he said "Oh! Thanks," and gave me a fraction of his normal smile. I got him some aroma therapy candles, his latest obsession, and that got him to smile just a little more.

As the days passed, he got worse. He had no idea where the toilet was and would get up in the middle of the night and pee wherever he thought the toilet was. It got really difficult. He was getting aggressive and had to be put in adult diapers. The room had to be lit so he knew where he was going. This meant moving him to the guest room to allow mom to catch some sleep. It was very unnerving. I kept waking up to check on him for fear that he might walk out of the house. He would look at me with a look that communicated that he had no idea what was happening and who I was. My heart broke every time I looked at him.

I didn't know what to do so I asked people. They advised speaking to a psychiatrist. I made an appointment with one and his advice was to just get him evaluated, or get his sugar levels down. "Bring him here," he said. Nothing he said made any sense to me, so I decided to speak to a doctor who had become a friend since we would refer clients to each other. Doctor Abel told me to get my dad's reports and meet him at 7 p.m.

My sister and I went. He looked through the papers and there, finally, he told me what I didn't want to hear: "This is not your Dada anymore. He has hepatic encephalopathy. The toxin build-up in his body is affecting the brain. Every time this happens, some of his brain gets irreparably damaged."

I think this was the moment when I started looking at the illness differently. The reality of the situation became more clear.

By the 1st of October, his mind was slightly clearer and he relented and said I could give him a bath. Dada was a proud man; no way, in any state of mind, would he be okay with me bathing him or changing his clothes. Now, however, he knew he needed the assistance. While bathing him, I found a wound on his big toe. Mom and I dressed it, but now there was another thing to worry about: His diabetes was likely too high. The fear got worse.

The next morning was a holiday. When I woke up, the first thing I did was, go to him. His breathing sounded laboured and every time I called out to him, he nodded his head but didn't open his eyes. As the minutes passed, even the nodding became feeble. Our first thought was to call the priest. That day was really the first time losing him became a reality. The priest came and gave him Extreme Unction. Everything around me seemed to be moving in slow motion. Time seemed to have just stopped and I couldn't seem to think straight. I could hear my heart beating in my head.

The air was heavy
All I could feel was fear;
I was horrified and scared
Death seemed too near.

This was a moment,
I had forever dreaded it;
My biggest fear forever,
It was near and I hated it.

What do we do?
All I need is to save him;
I wanted him to heal,
I wanted to protect him.

With each laboured breath
He was drifting away;
I just needed him here
I was not ready that day.

I called my sister in a panic. She said, "Call the ambulance." The ambulance took forever to come. That's how I felt at the time. It was actually there really quickly, but as I said, time was moving differently for me that day. The ambulance arrived with one female paramedic and a driver. We live on the third floor of a building that does not have an elevator. My mom's brother, Bernard, who moved close by, rushed over. So it was the driver, my friend Joanne, who was always there for me, my mom's brother and me who used all our might and got him slowly down to the ambulance. I had fractured my ankle two years prior and, on this day, I could feel that pain reverberating through me again as I struggled under his weight. "This is not happening," was all I could hear my mind repeat.

The ambulance ride was like something out of the worst-made movie. I could not stop looking at him lying there helpless. His eyes were shut and his body was moving to the movement of the vehicle. I could not wrap my head around the fact that there was no resistance from him. The vehicle moved and so did he. I was upset and I kept wanting to shake him and wake him and scream at him to snap out of it. "Come on Dada, stop this! Get up and let's get out of this thing!" That was all I wanted to say.

Accompanying someone in an ambulance on the streets of Goa brings out the worst emotions. No one cares that there may be an emergency careening towards them in the rear-view mirror; most just stayed where they were and drove the way they wanted to. The anger I felt at the insensitivity. I always make way for an ambulance, but no one on the road that day extended the same courtesy. My father needed to get to the hospital quickly and the world just lazed on by.

Since the ambulance people saw dad's condition, their choice of hospital was the one they thought would give us the best help. They took us to the Goa Medical College (GMC), the central hospital for the state. We have always heard that the best doctors were at GMC. At the end of the day, it is a government-run hospital and the number of people there was shocking. A horrible feeling permeated in that place.

They had no private rooms and wanted to put him in the ward. He was still completely unconscious and they shoved a feeding tube down his nose. I remember him gagging and throwing up and no one was there—just me and him—in the middle of this room that had loads of people being wheeled in and out in various stages of injury. People were screaming, some were speaking in hushed voices and the doctors looked like they had been on their feet for more than twenty-four hours. All I could do was cling on to Dada, the man who had been my rock. My silent cheerleader, now lying lifeless on a cold steel gurney.

They needed to run tests and, as we were instructed where to go, in voices that were a bit too stern for the situation we found ourselves in, we were told to accompany the patient at all times. I said, "Of course, where else would I be?"

Little did I know, they meant I had to ensure that he was moved from one machine to another and lifted onto the various tables by us, his family. So again, my best friend, my mom's brother and I took on the challenge of lifting him off his mobile gurney onto the CT scan machine and then in for an MRI. Lifting him in that state was difficult, both physically and emotionally. This was my Dada, the guy who would always be there to lift me up when I was down. Seeing him this way was beyond my comprehension. He was my support and now, here I was, being his. Taking on a role he used to play.

You were the hero,
The one who was strong;
I was the damsel
You took care of for long.

Suddenly life changed
Unconscious there you lay;
You needed my help
I'll not forget that day.

Suddenly the roles turned,
I was who was needed;
Your call for help,
I slowly conceded.

My mighty dad,
Strong and my protector
Now needed a hand:
Your helper, your daughter.

I just couldn't get over the fact that he just lay there. We could see slight movements and hear a few inaudible sounds he emitted, but other than that, there was nothing. No signs of life. His eyes were still shut tight. They moved him to the ward. I just stood there, exhausted and depleted but unable to move out of the space. I had to be there with him. I had to wait till he woke up. But my body had taken all the beating it could that day and my feet could no longer hold the weight of my body. So, reluctantly, I went home in the evening to get some rest, have a shower and get some food. We left a caretaker with him so that she could tend to him and call us if he needed anything.

I got home and tried to call her to find out if everything was under control. Her phone wasn't connecting, so I got back into the car fearing the worst and could not bear to think of what might have been going wrong. All my senses were heightened, worst-case scenarios shooting through my mind. I was five minutes away from the hospital but I felt like I was on a never-ending road.

A minute later, which seemed like an hour, the caretaker, sounding chirpy and nonchalant, called. Her phone was out of battery so she'd switched it off and put it to charge. I wanted to shout, laugh and cry, all at the same time. There was no point turning back, so I went to the ward and saw him still sleeping there peacefully. I gave his hand a little squeeze and left. I requested the care taker to message me and update me on his progress.

When I got home, my body completely slumped into a chair and there I sat, rooted till I was able to muster any strength to get myself to bed. As I walked to my room I got a call from the caretaker. She said the doctors wanted my consent to conduct a procedure on Dada at 4 a.m. No way was my mind or body going to cooperate at that hour, so I spoke to the doctor and gave consent. The caretaker, on a parting note, said "Oh! And Dada is coming around," and disconnected the phone. I didn't know if I was hearing things or if this was actually something she said. Thoughts flitted in my mind, one after the other: *Coming around? Could that be? No way... when I left, he was in a state of unconsciousness and nothing was rousing him.* Maybe it was my mind hearing what it wanted to hear.

I finally drifted off to sleep and turned and tossed all night. It had been one of those nights where your body was so exhausted that rest seemed too foreign an experience and thus, your body resists it. I took the next day off so I could be with Dada in the hospital. Mom was way too exhausted for another day in a place that was as emotionally draining as it was physically, so I asked her to stay home and accompany my sister in the evening during visiting hours. As with the previous night, the drive there took forever. I couldn't believe that it was the same hospital that, on normal days, took me fifteen minutes of travel time. I trudged up the corridors, dreading what was waiting for me. Maybe he was still lying there lifeless—oh! How I hated seeing him that way.

The elevator crept up to the fourth floor and, as I turned the corner to the ward, I saw a head moving around and in conversation on the bed that I had left him the previous day. To my utter shock and surprise, Dada was sitting up in bed having a hearty chat with his caretaker. This man always had the ability to completely shock me. I walked in coughing and, before I could ask what was going on and how he was feeling, he pulled me close and started rubbing my back. Before I could get my bearings he was already asking what was wrong and why I was coughing and what I was doing about it.

Always you before I
That's how he'd always be
Are you doing okay?
Don't you worry about me.

Always concerned for the other
Have you eaten? Did you sleep well?
But when we'd ask him,
"Hey, I'm doing swell."

Not a complaint would escape him,
Never would he say, "I'm ill,"
"I'm doing much better," was his answer
Till the end... still.

He made friends with all around him, concerned for everyone else and their wellbeing. When I was able to talk to him he said, "Oh! I'm doing so much better," and then he gave me a rundown of who was going through what and how serious everyone's issues were. I asked him if he was in pain and he said not at all. He told me he was only uncomfortable with "this damn tube in my nose". My classic Dada with his classic responses.

He was already set to leave the hospital. When the doctor came around for his rounds, that was the only thing he said. The doctor asked how he was doing; Dada responded that he was great—ready to go home. By the next day he was walking to the toilet on his own and utterly fed up with the hospital, as was I. It was just too loud and there was no privacy. Three days after we frantically admitted him to the hospital, he was out and ready to get back home. I remember it was a Saturday and my sister completed all the formalities and got him home. He was over the moon. He got home, showered and then went for his watering can to water his beloved plants.

It was so good to have him back home. I don't know why, but just his presence brought me a sense of safety and peace. All was right in the world again. Dada was back home, back in his own room and back doing all his favourite things. He pottered around, lit his scented candles and even came with us for Mass on the Sunday after. This was something he really yearned to do. He wasn't able to go for Mass often as his feet were swollen and painful, but that Sunday he said, "I'm coming."

Life got back to normal, but we noticed the wound on his foot wasn't tended to and seemed to have gotten worse. Mom got him to check his sugar levels, and it was off the charts. We called a new doctor and sent over the pictures. The doctor decided that he needed to be put on insulin and that we needed to take him for an evaluation. I took him to the doctor, who explained everything to him, and said that he needed to cut out a lot from his diet. I could see Dada getting annoyed and could tell that this doctor was another one struck off his list. However, this time, Dada did not fight back. He went with it.

The toe was getting worse, so a surgeon close to home decided to clean the wound and try to get it to heal. From that day on, we cleaned the wound and dressed it everyday. We checked his sugar levels often and made sure he had each of the three doses of insulin he needed per day. Finally the toe began to heal. Every little triumph felt like victory. I would press his feet every evening after work, dress the wound and have a little chat. That became our norm from the 6th of October.

On the 28th, the dark clouds started rumbling in again. We could see his mind slowly recede. This time he was completely agitated. He wasn't able to make sense of instructions and was not willing to stay in one place. I remember the sinking feeling. *Not another blow to the brain* was what I kept thinking. Patience and kindness were the only way. Even though it took half an hour to get him to use the washroom, we continued with calm voices and patient waiting.

My sister, my mother and I had to sit and make a decision. Do we take him back to the hospital or do we try to manage at home? We will do all we can at home, for after the last stint in the hospital, Dada had said, multiple times, that he never wanted to go back again. We hired a hospital bed and got a caretaker for him at home who was to join the next day. We moved my bed into the spare bedroom for him so he could have a safe and comfortable sleep that night before the hospital bed arrived.

When I got up in the morning, he was slightly better, less agitated but mumbling. It was difficult to rouse him and have a clear conversation with him. He was speaking, but to people who weren't there. He kept looking out of the window through the corner of his eye and saying something to someone I could not see. I heard words like mama and sister. His mother had passed away about ten years ago, and my grandmother's sister had been gone around eight. His mother's sister was a nun and we all called her Sister Flora. I just couldn't understand what he was saying and what was going on. Everyone else was running around the house trying to get things in order and arranged for dad. I just stood there taking in all his experiences.

Who did you see there?
What were they saying?
Were they preparing you
For where you were going?

The look in your eye scared me,
But you seemed so calm;
Whoever it was who was taking you,
I wanted to do them harm.

You were mine and I needed you,
I didn't want them to take you.
Why were they here already,
When I was not ready too?

It's such a universal mystery
When your loved one's at death's door,
They speak to their past ones,
While you are waiting on the floor.

It was such a surreal moment. I had been reading about this—visions of people who could not be seen, of those we lost before, coming to prepare our loved ones for the fate that awaited them. I never thought it would be such a real experience, something I still have so many questions about. I watched him have those weird conversations and something in me said, "NO! NOT YET." I started saying the Lord's Prayer—"Our Father," I began. In my head I said I'd say three Hail Marys, but every time I started the Hail Mary, I saw his lips curl in gentle repetition. So I carried on; I said the prayers out loud, I said them slowly, and every time I said the Holy Mary, he joined in with the first few words. Very slowly, his eyes began focusing again. I could see recognition, almost a smile crossing his lips. I told him, "Dada, I'll go get Chrystal,"

Dada responded, "Who?"
"My sister, your daughter!" I replied.

His next words stunned me: "Your sister? I wish I had sisters."

And he did—he had two sisters who he hadn't spoken to for years. It was a long story of miscommunications and misunderstandings that spanned almost a decade. Every time we tried to get them to speak, my Dada, with his pig-headed stubbornness, would vehemently deny that he had sisters and would break off the communication at that instant. Something inside me stirred. I had to make things right. I had to get him to make peace with his two sisters.

At this moment, however, all I cared for was getting him back on his feet. In about an hour, the hospital bed arrived at home, and the man we'd hired to care for Dada came and met him. Very slowly, as the day progressed, Dada came back to us. We had a bunch of holidays that week, so it was great to be right there with him. His smile was back, but he had slowed down further. We clicked a few pictures of him in his new hospital bed and he was super excited about it. He kept saying, "Oh! Lovely."

He enjoyed the prospect of having a convenient bed. I know that he was happier about the fact that it was convenient for everyone else. We didn't have to struggle to prop him up or to get him out of bed for a meal. It was all right there; the bed could be wound up so he could sit upright, and he enjoyed the liberation it gave him.

The next day his caretaker, a big burly guy, came to look after him. Dada had names for everyone; I was his shorty, and the caretaker soon became his gentle giant. As he generally would, Dada got talking to his "gentle giant" and before we knew it, he turned into his buddy. On the very first day, Dada was already telling me that the caretaker needed a holiday the following day for a festival. The caretaker took an instant liking to Dada as well and, for lunch on the very first day, he rushed home to get Dada some delicious local food cooked by his mom. That was Dada—a friend to everyone and loved by all. Dada was happy with his bed and he had company in his caretaker.

The 29th of October was when I called my cousin. I told her that Dada was not great and there might not be long to help her mother, our aunt—and my Dada rebuild those bridges. There was reluctance, as she didn't want her mom and our aunt to get hurt in case Dada again refused to speak to them. So I took on the mammoth task of convincing Dada to speak to them. At first I got a firm "No, thank you." I asked him again. The second time I said we didn't know what could happen.

I saw an understanding in his eyes, one that still warms my soul. It was an understanding I had always known—one that would come when I was struggling and didn't want to talk, or I was upset and had no words to describe. His line to me was, "But they didn't tell me about mama." Before his mom passed, he was not informed about how ill she was. He was told by a family friend and so he held this anger that he would not have got a chance to say goodbye to his beloved mom. Thankfully, he did reach on time, but that was the beginning of the end of his relationship with his sisters. Up until now, ten years later.

Your moral compass,
Your position of pride;
The way you'd stand by
And never hide.

For right was right
And wrong was wrong;
You held your integrity
Which was lifelong.

And when they didn't
Immediately inform you,
In your mind
They had wronged you.

I am glad
That bridge we did mend;
I am grateful
The talk was heaven-sent.

I called my cousin with the good news and we made the conversation happen. His first words, loud and clear "Hi, sister. Hi, my sister." My heart still skips a beat when I think of it. The three of them and their families spoke and it was a beautiful feeling. Ages had passed without them speaking and here we were, laughing and smiling and sharing the years that had flown by. Once we disconnected, Dada was smiling and seemed content. If there is one thing I will always be grateful for, it would be the persistence that was somehow inserted in me to get these grown-up kids to make nice. Help your loved ones rebuild bridges before it's too late. That is one less pang of guilt you do not need weighing you down.

The same evening, friends we'd had since my parents got married came over to see him. He was smiling and laughing and joking with them. At one moment, when the son of the couple and I were alone with Dada, out of the blue he said, "But now, whatever has to happen, I'm ready. I have no regrets." As he said the words I saw his eyes twinkle—they flicked to me and then back to the general direction he was looking in. The next few moments have been etched into my mind like an inscription on rock.

He kept looking at me out of the corner of his eye. "Make sure you don't put me in a bloody suit." As he said that I tried to tell him to stop talking, but something inside me said, *shut up and listen*. "I don't want them to put me in those gloves with a cross in my hands. Make sure my blanket is in there with me, and for God's sake, no brass band playing that moaning music." Saying that, he smiled. Neither the friend's son nor I could process that. I just looked at him and that glance said it all. After a short while he said he was quite tired. Everyone else came back into the room and we took some lovely pictures.

These were the friends we made our earliest memories with—weekends away as two young families, adventures we shared throughout: early trips to beach resorts in Mumbai, days spent in Goa visiting every spot and trying every cuisine, kids getting married and having babies of their own and both gentlemen enjoying the role of grandpa. Friends who Dada knew, for sure, would always be with us. He was definitely the kind who liked to have a great time and friends coming over were always met with days of planning what to do and where to take them for meals. This time, however, there was an unsaid agenda. Gordon and Annette, along with the kids, had to "say the best goodbyes".

The days following had some of his most treasured friends come over. A couple we met when he was at the peak of his career became ever so close and continued to stay in touch and visit as often as they could. Dada would call up his "Shawny boy" on weekends and the two would banter about anything and everything under the sun. The laughter they shared resonated through the house and every time we heard that laugh, mom and I knew he was talking to his good buddy Sean. His wife was also very fond of him and, while I was talking to her on her birthday and we were discussing Dada's illness she asked if we would mind them coming to see him. For some reason the words I uttered were "Come, say the goodbyes you have to." I think Suinta already planned her itinerary on hearing the word *come*.

By the 6th of November, both of them were here. They flew in just for a day and spent every waking hour with us, especially with him. Laughter and happiness resounded around the house till the last moments before they had to catch their flight. There was not a dry eye in the room. Sunita was bawling and holding dad. Under normal circumstances he would have asked her to stop it and to quit acting like a baby. But today, with moist eyes himself, all he said was, "Don't cry." Thus, the most special moments of 2024 had my wonderful Dada saying goodbye to the people he loved and appreciated most in the world. His constant friends. The people he could always count on.

The number of friends he had were plenty
Many when he was on top,
The number dwindled when he retired,
But with a few there was no stop.

In the moments we knew were to be his last,
A few could have come to say,
The goodbyes they wished that never came,
For he passed in a few days.

Those that mattered came willingly;
They showed him how they cared.
He went away with a heart full of love,
And so to walk away he dared.

They still are with us strong and clear,
Of this he knew they would
He left us knowing they'd stay with us,
So drift slowly he could.

During the night, I'd wake up very often just to check on him. On some of those nights I'd see him moving his hands erratically towards the sky trying to push something away. Well that happened once. On other days, I saw him reaching upward and trying to draw something toward him. One night, I walked in and saw him petting an invisible pet that seemed to be lying on his tummy. It was a very serene moment and till this day, something that I can't explain. The internet explained that the first bit was a moment of terminal agitation and then the rest, death bed visions. It was scary but also calming all the same. Did he see people who were welcoming him to his eternal home? To a lay person the reactions would seem strange, but now in retrospect, it is extremely reassuring knowing that something was keeping him calm. In his waking moments too, both mom and I actually heard him have very peaceful conversations with someone. When we asked who he was speaking to he just said, "no one" with a peaceful look on his face.

The day after Sunita and Sean left, his health started declining. Earlier, he could get up unassisted, but that day his feet were not responsive to his command. However, he went up to the terrace that day and sat on his swing looking at his potted plants. He told his caretaker how to arrange the plants for him, and when he got back he looked drained. Despite his exhaustion, he stayed in the living room with mom and me. He usually never sat there while we watched television but this night he stayed. I was so happy with how the whole day went because he did so much. The fact that his feet were not cooperating was not even something I thought about. For me, that was the day he did it all. But that was the calm before the storm. The next day, the storm had arrived and threw us all.

Sunday morning, we were to go for mass and keep Dada in the charge of the caretaker. However, something didn't feel right. So I went and picked up breakfast for us all and came home as soon as I could. Dad's feet kept giving way as the caretaker brought him to the table. Slowly, he battled with that spoon but ate his favourite Indian breakfast of *upma*. When he finished, he wanted to return to the room. We asked him to sit up a bit, but he was adamant. He was too tired, he said. So we took him in. After about 15 minutes, we heard him call for the caretaker, and we all ran in to see that he had puked. He was so embarrassed and upset. We assured him it was absolutely fine and went about trying to clean him up.

While the caretaker cleaned the room, mom and I decided to help him change his clothes. As we were doing this, mom and I were shocked to see a wound around his tailbone: He had developed a bed sore. I asked the caretaker when this appeared and he said he noticed it a few days ago when bathing him. That completely infuriated me and I rushed to the pharmacy to get some medicine for him. They didn't have the Cavalon spray that the caretaker had recommended so I came home with another ointment that the pharmacist told me would work. I called my sister, who rushed in. We immediately went to the city and went to every pharmacy there. Finally, we got the spray. Thus began the nightmare of the bedsore.

That day, I turned Google upside down to find an immediate cure. The best I could find was to get him an air mattress that would stop the spread. So I ordered it immediately and it was to arrive the very next day. The day prior, mom had ordered a walking stick for Dada—one that he never got around to using and, in fact, still stands in a box behind the door of the room he was in. I could see my vivacious, happy, energetic Dada dwindling, suffering, and that was more than my heart could take.

The caretaker got him out of the room in the afternoon and he sat on his beloved chair. His baby girl, our cocker spaniel Lexie, was lying by his feet with her head resting on him. Dada sat with his head back and eyes closed. I have a picture of him perched there. His music was playing in the room. He struggled his eyes open and said to me, "Tell the band to play 'My Way'." And he put his head back and closed his eyes again. I asked Siri to play his song and his fingers drummed ever so slightly. Dada loved karaoke and his favourite song to perform was "Quando, Quando, Quando" by Engelbert Humperdinck. I played that song next and gently cajoled him to sing along. Even at that level of fatigue he tried and actually stayed on key. I have a video of that too—the last conscious memory of a man that gave me his all.

To see you slip away
And close your eyes,
Made me question
Rethink all the lies

I told myself repeatedly,
"He'll definitely be okay."
I thought you'd bounce back
Like you did the previous day.

Who knew this was it
The last I'd hear you sing;
Who knew the end was here,
That day you passed on your wedding ring.

# CHAPTER 3

# THE BEGINNING OF THE END

Yes, I have dedicated an entire chapter to the last one week. Why? Because that was the week that changed my entire life forever. No other period of my forty-year existence made such an impact on me, including the time I fractured my leg and had surgery for the same. This was the week that would forever be the most emotional, physically draining and impactful week of my life—where I grew as a person and broke as a daughter. This was the week that reminded me of the profound love I was fortunate enough to receive from my beloved Dada, and reminded of the deep love and admiration I still had for him.

The Sunday that I spoke about, before he got bad, I informed him about a doctor coming to see him on Monday.

"No, I don't want to meet any doctor," he said stubbornly.

"Dada, please. Just let him check your condition," I pleaded, but to no avail. He just shook his head in a clear 'no'. I took a deep breath before changing my tactic. "At least tell me why you don't want to meet the doctor."

"I don't want to go back to the hospital. I never want to go to any hospital again." He didn't elaborate, and he didn't need to. The memory of his recent hospitalisation was still fresh.

I took his hand in mine. "Dada, I will not let that happen. I promise."

He was silent for a moment. "What if the doctor insists?"

"I'll ask the doctor to leave," I promised and meant it.

Maybe it was the look on my face or the determination in my eyes, but he believed me and agreed.

By Monday, Dada was only responding in grunts. He was responding to his name, but only by nodding. Never again did I hear his signature "Yeah, darling" in response to my "Dada". Mom messaged me in the morning after I had gone to work and said that he wasn't opening his eyes and would not be able to get out of bed. I remember telling her not to worry, that he must be tired. I assured her that in a while, he would get up for breakfast. That was an assurance that I made, but it wasn't to be. The caretaker made him sit up in bed and they slowly tried to give him some juice, which he managed to consume. I told mom that we need to keep him hydrated and healthy.

When I got home from work I made him a soft scrambled egg and he ate that quite nicely. I was happy—it seemed like he was snapping out of this. The doctor came in and checked him. He told us to feed him liquids and fruit in juiced form. He also changed some of his medications and prescribed medicines for twenty days. That was such a relief to hear. The doctor was giving him at least twenty days. We were instructed to continue giving him his insulin and get an air mattress for the bed sore. I told him it was already on its way.

The mattress arrived soon after and luckily my mom's brother Bernard, who has been a rock for us and visited Dada every week this year, came by for his weekly visit. He set up the mattress and laid him back on his bed. Dada looked so comfortable.

Every night before going to bed, before Dada lost consciousness, I'd kiss him on the forehead and say, "Goodnight Dada, see you tomorrow," and he'd say, "Good night, darling, thank you for everything." I'd never say *you are welcome* and instead responded with, "Don't be silly." That night, I did the same, but got no response. So I bent closer to his ear and told him I loved him and that he was my hero. I told him that he was the only one who could drive me insane and still have my heart. Then I said something I wanted to say for a long time: "I'm sorry, Dada, sorry for all the times I may have hurt you or disappointed you." At that moment, a tear rolled down his cheek. I knew he could hear me. So I continued: "Thank you. Thank you for all you have done for me, all the love you gave me and all the experiences you ensured I had." I thanked him for everything and more. I did this every night till I ran out of nights.

Your eyes were closed
To the world outside;
Your mind was still
Right by my side.

Words I whispered
You heard, I'm sure;
I told you I loved you
I know you know.

For every moment
Was a moment lost;
I needed to thaw
All the years of frost.

But by your side,
As we reached the finish line,
I felt your love and finally
You felt mine.

Since Dada enjoyed the scrambled egg the previous night, I made one for him for breakfast the next day too. That day led to something my mom could not handle, but adrenaline helped her through. Dada started having loose motions. The caretaker and mom could barely handle it. There was no stopping it. They tried to get him to the bathroom, but his legs weren't working anymore. So, the caretaker had to almost drag him. As he was held up, mom washed him thoroughly.

My Dada, the strong, proud man who would not like to be made a fuss over when he was ill, had to be washed and cleaned and had to use diapers. The caretaker blamed me for giving him the egg, and I had no energy to argue. All I wanted to do was be there for my Dada. Though he was barely conscious, he resisted me changing his diaper when the caretaker left. I told him to stop resisting. He has done this for me when I needed it as a baby, and now it was my turn. Immediately I felt him stop resisting. I cleaned him and put on his diaper again.

The caretaker was acting up, as most of them often do. He would come in late and my Dada would be waiting for breakfast, hungry but uncomplaining. Wednesday was uneventful in the morning but then, in the afternoon, mom called, saying that he was bleeding from the mouth. I went into panic mode and rushed home. I was shaking by the time I got there. When I went to see him, I realised that his dentures, still in his mouth, were cutting through his cheek. It didn't help that the caretaker kept putting him on his side to avoid the bed sore from rubbing against the mattress, which was not required because of the air mattress but the caretaker would not listen. While on his side, the denture hurt the insides of his mouth. We made him sit up and managed to get the dentures out. Since it was superficial bleeding, we rinsed his mouth and I returned to work.

Dada did not seem happy when the caretaker was around. Plenty of times his eyes would shoot open and he would glare at him. The moment one of us would go to him and stand in his line of vision, his stare would soften and he'd close his eyes. When I got home on Wednesday evening, he was calm and lying on his back. He seemed the most comfortable when he was on his back. We fed him some buttermilk and juice a while later and called it a night. Every morning at about 4:20 a.m., both mom and I would wake up and go straight to his bedside. A quick thirty seconds and then head back to bed. That became the routine.

Thursday was mind-boggling. We had an event in school. The teachers were performing for the children and I was participating in a play. As we were getting ready to get on stage I got a frantic call from mom: the caretaker hadn't turned up. It was already 11 a.m. and there was no sign of him. Every time I called him, his phone went unanswered. I finished the performance and ran home. Mom and I tended to Dada. We fed him, gave him a sponge bath, and then changed his clothes.

All day we worked tirelessly and made sure he was comfortable and at peace. Even though his eyes were closed I knew he was aware of every little thing going on around him. Every time I spoke to him he seemed to know. Every time I held his hand I could feel a slight pressure from him. Every time I moved him I felt like he was trying to help. Usually, getting him to move positions was very difficult, but on this particular day, it all just seemed easy.

The caretaker said he was at some religious celebration and that he would send someone over the next day. I felt extremely helpless thinking about the day ahead, but mom and I decided to take it one moment at a time. So that's what we did, and it felt easy.

Having you alone to ourselves
Was a time we really did need;
Being able to do for you what was needed
To care for you and to feed.

Those moments, though very difficult,
Where spiritually for us placed;
There wasn't a single moment then
That was remotely a waste.

For every minute was special,
And every second perfect;
I just wish you were speaking,
So you'd know my love and how I meant it.

Even though it was difficult, it was the most important day we spent with dad. Every second we had with him just seemed spiritual. In that moment all I felt was plain, unadulterated love. He was my dad—the one who picked me up and put me over his shoulders when I was small; the one who would make me laugh out loud and could sooth my deepest pain with a smile. When we drove around alone, we always had the best conversation. He made me feel special; in his presence I felt heard. Here I was, trying my best to be a sliver of how compassionate he had always been to me. It tore at my heart that I couldn't speak to him and have him respond. There was still so much I wanted to ask and tell him, but it was a one-sided conversation.

Throughout the day that's all we did: tend to him, talk to him and listen to his favourite music with him. That evening, as mom sat beside him and Engelbert Humperdinck sang away, I heard him say his last complete and clear word. Mom left his hand for a split second to do something at the foot of the bed. As clear as day I heard him say, "JENNIFER." My mom's name was the final utterance. He would tell people he loved her when she wasn't around and pick on her when she was. On this day, it was clear that she was his forever.

The next day, the caretaker sent in a substitute—a very thin man who seemed very gentle and kind. I immediately felt like Dada was in safe hands with him. I took a day off to lend as much support as I could give. Our first order of business was to change his clothes and bathe him. So the new guy and I held him up. As he stood with his arms on my shoulders, I was facing him. At that moment, I said to him "Look Dada, we are dancing!" His eyes shot open and he smiled. My heart leapt with joy but it was short-lived.

Once we got him into a chair, his body slumped and I supported him with the weight of my own body while the caretaker gently sponged him. When we were done, we got him dressed and upright in bed for some sustenance. He consumed some juice and some unsweetened lassi, into which we mixed his meds. Every time I put the cup to his lips and said, "Swallow, Dada," he did.

Both mom and I were waiting for him to just wake up. My sister, Chrystal, was to leave for Abu Dhabi the next day. In my head I was praying that we would not lose him while she was away. The whole of Friday, Dada slept peacefully, as the caretaker sat beside him listening to scriptures all day. Dada seemed so much at peace. Mom and I took some time off and rested too, as the night prior—and for the entire week—we had been on our feet constantly. By afternoon we were rested enough to take on anything we had to, but that wasn't required. He was completely at peace lying there, co-operating when he had to be cleaned and fed. Again we sat by him and put on his favourite music.

Holding his hand through this week was very calming for me. It was something that I did automatically. I would hold his hand in mine and memorise how it felt, how it looked and how his fingers were similar to mine. Yes, I wanted him to feel me holding his hand so that he would be assured that I was near, but I did it more for myself. I wanted to feel him and hold on to him as much as I could. I wanted to hold on forever and never let go. Today, when I close my eyes and go back to that week, I can still almost feel his hand in mine.

Saturday morning, the original caretaker was back. I told him to just leave Dada on his back as he looked peaceful in that position. He had some juice and some vegetable broth and settled in for the day. In the evening, my sister's ex-husband—my niece, Maegan's father—was supposed to arrive in Goa. He touched down, dashed over to his place for a shower and was home to see his favourite person. I asked Dada to open his eyes—Val was here.

Dada made a sound and then something I had been dreading happened. I heard a raspy, fluid sound when he took his breath. I had been reading up on his medical condition all along and that sound scared me. I took mom out of the room and, for the first time, I articulated the words I had dreaded saying: "Doesn't look like we have much time left." Neither mom nor I wanted to believe that, but the signs were there.

Dada had always been very fond of my niece's father. Very often, they would go on long drives together. It felt like Dada had waited for him to come back so he could begin to let go.

A week prior, an old friend's son from Mumbai, Shrenik, had called Dada, knowing nothing about his condition. That old friend had unfortunately passed away just a few months prior. The son was always fond of Dada and called to check on him out of the blue. I told him about dad's condition and he promised to come see him. He was travelling for work all week but that Saturday he called to say he would come on Monday. Something in me blurted out, "I don't think we have till then."

Before I knew it, this guy hopped on a plane and was at our doorstep. He arrived at about 11 p.m. Shrenik, my niece Maegan, and I stayed up at Dada's bedside reminiscing. We spoke about old times and how Shrenik lovingly called Dada "Laughful Uncle". We told Maegan how we all became friends and Shrenik shared moments when Dada inspired him. Through all this chit chat, Dada's breathing had gone back to normal. He was definitely listening and smiling right through.

The night before was like
A scene from a movie;
Laughter filled the air
Not a moment gloomy.

Though we all knew
Time was not on our side,
We kept love and laughter loud
Our sorrow we tried to hide.

It was a night that I'll remember
Till I take my last breath—
The night before you were taken
By the angel of death.

All your wishes granted—
That was all we could do;
For never would you need to ponder,
"Was our love for you true?"

Everything was just simple perfection. I decided to sleep by his bedside that night. I set up a foldable bed next to him and lay down beside him by 1:00 a.m. I clutched his hand all night. Most of the night I could feel him holding my hand back. At 3:30 a.m., I had moved my hand away in my sleep and I heard him make a sound and the rasp was back. I woke mom up and we both sat by his side till he calmed down and settled back in at 4:00 a.m. I held his hand again and drifted into a sleep that didn't break till 8:00 a.m.—the latest I had slept in months.

I woke in a panic and when I went out everyone was up and awake. I brushed and showered and went back to my vigil beside his bed. Mom joined me and we sat there, holding his hands and speaking softly to him. I could hear the rasp and it was unnerving. When mom went out to get something, I whispered in Dada's ear for the last time, "If you are too weak and you can't do this any longer, let go Dada. I'll take care of everything." How I thought I could live up to that tall promise, I will never know. I said the words for him to hear, but I didn't really mean them. I still needed my Dada, I still need him even now and I think I will always need him.

My closest friend, Joanne, who was there for every bit of everything we went through as a family, returned this sunny, bright Sunday. She was always there, always around, always someone whom Dada would come out to entertain and have a laugh with. He'd brighten up when she would visit and, with the broadest smile, say, "Hey Jo!" Joanne joined mom and me as we took our seats around dad.

At 11:10 a.m., Shrenik told us he was going to take a nap, and so mom decided we could hear Sunday Mass online. We set up the speaker beside Dada and began listening to the Mass. Sunday Mass was something Dada never missed. Even when he was working and would get home at 2 and 3 a.m. on a Saturday, we would all be trooped off for Sunday Mass. When he was too ill to travel, he would make mom put on the online Mass and he would listen and participate wholeheartedly.

That Sunday was a bit different. His eyes were closed but he was present. After the second reading, Dada took a deep breath and I stood up and looked at him. I urged him to let the breath out. Slowly, he did and I breathed a sigh of relief. Then the Acclamation began. The Alleluia is something he would sing as loud as he could, but that day, he took a second deep breath. This time it took longer for him to release it. Before the Alleluia ended, he took his last breath, and as that breath gently left his lips I could feel my soul crumble.

In that moment, softly, steadily, during the holy celebration of Sunday Mass, he heeded my advice and let go. I instinctively looked at my watch. 17th of November, 11:36 a.m., on a beautiful Sunday morning—his favourite day of the week. One day before the day he became a father for the first time, forty-four years ago.

Everything seems so poetic
Now, in retrospect;
In that moment of your last breath,
I felt only love and respect.

Like the breath of an angel,
Soft and gentle in the breeze,
You let go of all your pain—
You slipped away with ease.

The whole world stood still for a moment,
Everything around me stopped;
In that moment it was just us—
And then that moment popped.

Chaos was then unleashed—
Were you still there or gone forever?
I put my ear to your chest;
The silence I will forget... never.

The moment I have always feared was upon me and, in that space, everything stood still. The sounds in my head were so loud, but around me there was just silence. The moment passed and then, pandemonium. My mother's scream pierced through my mind, as shrill and sharp as the invisible knife I felt cutting through my heart. People were screaming at me for directions and I could just stand rooted to the ground. Looking at him, lying there like he was in a peaceful sleep, I gently lowered myself to his chest and heard silence. I felt his skin, cool under my touch, and slowly my own heartbeat in my ear yanked me out of my head and into reality.

Dada was gone.

# CHAPTER 4

# THE IMMEDIATE AFTERMATH

"Shall I call the ambulance?" Joanne asked. I feebly nodded a yes. Before I knew it people started talking all at once. Shrenik came out and said something, and Maegan and her father returned and were asking me things, and all I could do was switch on autopilot. The ambulance finally arrived and I was still standing in the same spot where I was when he breathed his last. The paramedic put the stethoscope to his chest and asked, "Shall we take him to the hospital?"

"No," I said, almost snapped at her. "What is happening? Is there a pulse?"

She told me they needed a doctor to declare. I asked again, "Is there a pulse?" and she shook her head. No. That was it. His heart had stopped while mine continued to drum on in my chest. His heart was silent, while mine continued to beat. His heart had ceased to work and it broke off a small piece of my own heart while it did.

I don't remember when I started crying, but my face was soaked in tears as, with trembling hands, I dialled his first-born, my sister, who was in a different country. The one who made him a Dada forty-four years ago on the very next day, the 18th. The one who gave him his proudest title of "DADA". Before I said the words, I'm sure she knew by the look on my face. I saw her face contort and then that scream again. She wanted to see him and I panned the phone to face him. I heard her sob and felt myself sob along. How could this larger-than-life human lie here motionless? How could he have left this world so soon? We used to joke that he would put us all in our graves. He would always say he had longevity in his family—his mom died at ninety-six—here he was a mere seventy-four years old.

Being a Sunday, and being Goa, no doctor was willing to come over. The paramedic stayed with us very kindly, saying all the right things and giving us tips on who to call and how to go about this. I just wanted all the buzzing to stop and to be left alone with my dad. I wanted to hold him and scream and completely break down, but no one was leaving and everyone just wanted to keep moving.

The medical fraternity lost my respect that day. A doctor we visited since we were children let me down. "I don't do home visits," he said. Someone who had treated all of us through our childhood and teens, the person who Dada would trust whole heartedly, the one who would always assure us that our health was safe in his hands, decided that his one Sunday was too important to forgo.

Out of everyone present who was trying to get hold of a doctor, Shrenik, someone who has never lived in Goa, managed to find someone to come in on Justdial. Nothing about that time is clear in my memory except how Dada's face looked. Peace. Calm. His lips slowly lost their colour and I remember thinking: this is ridiculous. So many people flooded in, offering condolences and words of comfort while he was still lying there. We prayed around him and the priest came and said another prayer. People kept shoving phones into my hand and all I did was listen and respond with a yes or no. The Goan Rites called, the ambulance service called, relatives were calling.

All I wanted was to get our family dog, Lexie, to say bye to her favourite human. I got her up on the bed on which he lay and she sniffed him, not knowing what was going on around her, except that something bad was happening. She looked scared and very confused. It seemed like he lay there for hours, but it apparently wasn't that long. The house was still full of people when the hearse van came. I could feel my body fight within itself. All at the same time I wanted to throw myself over him and not let them take him away, and yet I needed to make sure his final exit from the home he built and loved was carried out with dignity.

This was the final time
You'd ever go out that door—
A frame that you built
With dedication, hard work and more.

Everything had to be perfect;
Your shelves had no dust.
But now you were embarking,
And this was your final dusk.

A home you wanted so bad,
You built it from your heart;
You filled its rooms so beautifully
And cared for it with all your love.

And now you bid it farewell;
All your work left behind.
People with hearts so empty—
Hearts that wanted time to rewind.

I followed him to the hearse, whispering a prayer and a parting thank you. Once I got back to the apartment, the gaping wound was now bare—an empty, hollow space that felt both numb and excruciatingly painful at the same time. I kept walking around—Standing still or sitting in place created too much space to think. Thinking was beyond my capability. Stuck in a loop, I kept replaying every moment of that morning.

Did I know he was leaving today? Maybe some sixth sense did, or I would not have slept by his bedside. So many questions suddenly started intruding. Funeral arrangements needed to be made. Would we have to call different people? What coffin would we get? What flowers? What about his clothes? How will the Mass be organised? Would we live-stream the service? There were just so many decisions to be made and, considering we have never ever had to do this before, we relied on our friends and family to help—and help they did.

Melanie, our one stop for everything, was already on the phone getting arrangements done. She's been a family friend for ages and we have seen a number of amazing highs and devastating lows together. Mel always has her checklists, and all I was really meant to do was nod yes or no and call my sister if I didn't have an answer for any question.

The thought of the funeral made me nauseous. I didn't want to be standing there with all those people telling me he was such a great guy. I knew he was a great guy. I knew and loved him all my life! But life was so unfair. He was just seventy-four. He had so much more living to do... I couldn't stay still. They kept saying I needed to eat. I didn't want to eat, I didn't want to sleep—I just wanted time to rewind so I could say more to him. I wanted to keep talking to him and holding his hand, but he was no longer here. I walked around aimlessly, smoked more than I should have, and cried.

Oh, how I cried. I always thought of myself as being the kind who just couldn't allow my tears to flow. The real me suddenly awoke. The memories of times I was nonchalant or irritable with him kept plaguing my mind, and I couldn't shake the first feeling: **guilt**. Though I know how every relationship has its ups and downs, and every human feels those negative emotions, I just couldn't think of anything else. I kept saying sorry and people kept reminding me of how human and natural our relationship was. They kept trying to remind me of all I was to him. No words were believable enough for me.

My Dada was my hero. He always wanted the best for me. There were times I would sit and wonder how selfless he was. His first instinct, when he sat to eat, would be to give us a taste or to ask if we wanted some. He was the kind who would always ask about our days and make sure we were taken care of. Right till his last breath, I believe he decided how he would go and when, so that we were not put to any inconvenience. And then there was me, the one with a temper, that would get into idiotic squabbles with the man who gave me his all.

On the day he passed and the day after, I felt like the wind had been knocked out of me. All I wanted was to wake up from this dreadful nightmare, but it just never happened, no matter how hard I tried. My Dada was not coming back, and I had to live with that knowledge for the rest of what remains of my life. In my conscious stupor I walked to the window where his most beloved plant sat and, in my head, I said, "I miss you and want you back." At that instant a beautiful white butterfly with yellow splotches flew past and lingered a bit. Coincidence. That was the first and only thought in my mind.

The feeling in my chest was weird—like an itch that couldn't be scratched, a weight that was weightless; like there was something dark inside that completely clouded my every thought and emotion. I was numb and yet felt the wretched pangs of despair. I was hollow and yet so full of emotion. All I had now were pictures on my phone. I kept scrolling; I took mom's phone and sent myself all she had. I took dad's phone and opened his gallery hoping to do the same. The first picture in his gallery broke me all over again. There I was, preoccupied with the coffee in front of me. I'll get back to this bit later.

That phone was like a treasure trove—pictures we had no idea he clicked. His phone gallery, like him, overflowed with love for his girls. He always boasted about being the only man in a house full of women. My heart then knew that his heart knew that he was loved. Loved to the point that made him "the happiest guy in town".

So much sorrow you left behind,
Hearts wrenched out of place;
Torn in shambles we were left—
Survival would be God's grace.

How could we move on without you?
That was a lofty task.
Do we pretend we are okay after?
Does the world want a mask?

You were so much more than known
To all who walked on by;
You were the centre of our lives
Our anchor always, our only guy.

Everything was so weird around me. I couldn't understand how to put one foot in front of the other and I was told I had to give the eulogy. It felt like one sucker punch after another. How are human beings supposed to do this? Your heart is ripped apart, your mind has ceased to function, and now you have to reach within and find words to celebrate a life that made you who you are—and now it's gone. But that's okay, the human mind is resilient! Just hunker down and do it. *Urgh!!* Society and its pressure. There is only so much nonsense a person can take, and on this day I reached my limit. As usual, I said nothing.

Everyone around me kept telling me what to do and how to do it. Though it might seem like a complaint, at that time that is what I needed, for I could not function on my own no matter how hard I tried. My sister was arriving the same evening, and that would entail another round of ugly tears and pain. Annette and Gordon came back immediately from Mumbai and they were our life lines. Mom, Maegan, Chrystal and I would have completely crumbled otherwise. As I said earlier, the next day was Chrystal's birthday and Dada would not have wanted us to be in complete shambles, so we decided to have the funeral on the 19th of November instead. That first night without him was surreal. I woke up again at 4 a.m. and went to check on him, realised he was not there and broke down again. I hoped so badly that I would wake up and he would be in his room on his hospital bed.

I can't even remember the 18th. I didn't know what to say to her. How do I wish her a *happy birthday*, when this day was the furthest thing from happy? So I just hugged her and we cried again. Mom, Chrys, Maegan and I were like four islands floating on the same ocean of despair, not colliding but drifting by each other in our own daze. I don't remember eating or sleeping. Nothing else seemed real, just the empty void inside our chests. All day I wrote and rewrote my eulogy. Every time I read it aloud I cried all-consuming, body-shuddering tears and I was supposed to deliver this in front of the congregation at a Mass that was being streamed live the following day.

There was a steady stream of visitors, all telling us about how amazing he was and how he helped them in some way or another. What can anyone say to that? We could muster feeble thank-yous, but other than that our minds were still grappling with words. The feelings were real and raw. Every corner of the house reminded us of him. That day, for the first time since we moved into this place, I took a short three-minute drive to the cemetery. A small, isolated space, marked with not more than eight crosses, was where my Dada was going to rest. I looked around at the names on the crosses around the space dug out for him. Neither name nor face was known to any of us. Now Dada would forever be in this space and I didn't know how to feel about that. Peaceful? Yes it was. Isolated? Definitely. Derelict? Yes, I did not like that, but I decided to do my best to make it look good since this was his resting place now and here is where he would be..

I didn't want to handle the funeral arrangements. The undertakers sent me pictures of coffins and flower arrangements and lists of things that would go in the coffin with him. I sent the pictures to Chrystal and asked her to decide, which she did immediately along with the flower arrangement on the coffin. All else, I sat with a pencil and decided. He had already told me what he wanted so I had an idea. He didn't want those "damn white gloves", so I crossed that out. No new rosary—he would have his own wrapped around his hands. Just making those arrangements was more than enough. I needed to take a nap after that. But no way did sleep find me. The discomfort of it all was too much to bear.

To think of these things
I never would;
It just was something
I thought I never should.

All of my life
This was my biggest fear—
To lose a loved one,
Someone so dear.

Now here I sat,
Pencil in hand,
Making the arrangements
Of a funeral plan.

How was I supposed to
Be okay with this,
When the person in the coffin
I already, painfully missed?

I could not sleep that night. I hated every moment. I walked around till late and then finally just lay in bed. I didn't want to acknowledge the heaviness of what the next day would bring. My workplace flew the flag at half-mast and the dispersal time was advanced so more colleagues could attend. Breakfast was forced on me like every meal since. Maegan ironed Dada's red shirt and beige trousers while I polished his shoes. Chrystal and Joanne made all the other arrangements and ensured that everyone was fed. We had to make arrangements for food and snacks—what would be served outside the church, and all the other stuff that I just couldn't handle. The most daunting thought in my head was that this was going to be the absolute last time I would ever see him in the flesh. I couldn't imagine not seeing him everyday. I have not been away from him for more than a month at a time my whole life.

# CHAPTER 5

# The Final Goodbye

It took me more than two weeks to get back to this part of my narration because, for me, this was probably the worst and most difficult day of my entire life. As the clock ticked on, the dreaded hour approached. Visitors were in and out. My sister's ex-husband was kind enough to volunteer to handle all the morgue arrangements. Unlike many other places, the morticians in Goa prep the person at the morgue itself. It is mandatory that a family member be present throughout. I will forever be grateful to Valentine for shouldering this unbearable responsibility, especially since he was so fond of Dada, and Dada was so fond of him. I can't imagine how difficult that must have been.

We got dressed—None of us wanting to wear black, because that was what Dada didn't want, but not feeling drawn to any other colour.

The day was surreal, like snippets flashing by in a dream-like depiction from a movie. We got into my friend's car and waited outside the church. I didn't know what to expect or how to react, so I just let go. I couldn't hold my emotions so tightly anymore—it wasn't doing me any good. As we stood there, I looked up at the road and saw the hearse van driving in. That was the moment I felt my breath catch in my chest and my entire being unravel. It was a feeling I had never anticipated, never known before, an overwhelming flood to my senses. Every part of me went into absolute, immediate panic.

As the hearse van backed into the entrance and the doors swung open, I got the first glimpse of the casket we had so lovingly chosen—the final resting place for my beautiful, caring, loving, always laughing and happy Dada.. I still hear the sound of the wood being pulled out of the van, and I remember all us—close family—walking behind it as they carried him down the aisle to the altar for the last time.

I stood rooted to a spot beside that beautifully crafted piece of wood, waiting for them to reveal my Dada's face, yet hoping that I didn't have to see him like that. But then they opened the lid and I broke even further. There he lay, more peaceful than I'd seen him in months. I expected other things but rather, here he was in front of us, looking like he was in a peaceful sleep, but also looking as naughty as always—there seemed to be a slight smirk at the corner of his lips.

Here lay the man who made me who I am today. He taught me how to be strong in the face of adversity and that integrity was everything. He showed me that true leadership meant compassion and carrying the equal weight of your employees and anyone you worked with. He taught me that building people up for the good of the collective was more important than tearing people down for individualistic pleasures and ego boosts. Here lay the best example of a leader, a friend, a family man and, of course, a father, I have ever known.

For an hour we got to say our goodbyes, to hold him, to feel what his skin felt like for the last time. I wasn't prepared for how it would feel—so familiar, yet colder than it had ever been. His skin and the upper flesh was soft and life-like, but beneath that was stiffness. We stood around him, saying goodbye. We smiled at how peaceful he looked and joked about how I used to call him "Popsicle" sometimes and now here he was. It might seem insensitive to the reader but that was how Dada was. He would never have given up the opportunity to make that joke.

After our private hour with him, people started pouring in—friends, acquaintances, relatives, colleagues, employees. All sombre and shocked that they were there to say goodbye to the man who had always been "full of life." The irony was them saying it beside his coffin. Many were in tears, mourning the loss of the man who raised me. The presence of some angered me—those who had known he was ill and didn't care enough to come and visit him when he was still alive, now flooding social media with eulogies and expressions of sorrow. Why do we appreciate a person only after they are gone? Why don't we express that love when they are here? Of course, the church was also filled with those who stayed in touch right through and undeniably felt the pain of losing such a wonderful friend, colleague and boss.

It irked me that people were moving his hair or talking too loudly, but then I realised, he touched so many hearts and they were all here because of that impact and all had the right to say goodbye.

The day I dreaded
Was finally here.
There was sadness all over,
And many a tear.

The impact you had
Was so clear to see;
The church had no floors,
Just a human sea.

You lay there as usual,
Still owning the room;
The congregation looked at you
Like an admirable groom.

You looked very dapper
In your combo of red and cream,
And though all was peaceful,
I really wanted to scream.

Don't go, Dada—
I'm not ready yet.
Some live till 90,
74 was all you get.

And as we all bid you farewell,
There was not a dry eye.
All I kept thinking was 'no,'
And I kept wondering why.

The service began and the main celebrant was my mom's cousin, Fr. Lionel, and oh, what a service it was. I didn't think I'd be able to pay attention, but I hung on to every word. Dada was so beautifully celebrated that day. The essence of who he was came through so clearly and beautifully. Every word he said about my loving Dada was so true. Some of my colleagues, who had just met Dada in passing, came up to me later and expressed how the Mass was like an introduction to a really special man.

Then Chrystal went up accompanied by her band members and sang the song he demanded: "My Way". She sang it so beautifully that not a dry eye was left in that congregation. The clarity in her voice reverberated through the church and shook me to my core. The melody and lyrics were a perfect farewell to the man that was. No regrets, just a life well and fully lived.

After that song, it was my turn to go up and deliver my eulogy. I didn't want to after the song. I could barely breathe, let alone speak. As I walked to the microphone, all I could do was look at Dada lying there. Everyone else in the congregation seemed to have disappeared and it was only us, father and daughter: one speaking, the other listening intently.

There were moments I had to stop and catch my breath, but it had to be clear and perfect. It took me back to moments when he had helped me prepare for a speech I had to give or an elocution I was participating in. Dada was always great with his words and strong in delivery. I felt the intense need to make him proud, even then. The man, the vision, the voice—I wanted everyone present to know how special he was. I wanted them to know why he chose to wear what he wore for his final appearance. I wanted them to know how deeply he loved mom, how passionate he was about being a grandfather and how impeccable he was as a dad. My voice wavered often, but I kept going. When I was done, I walked down, kissed him, placed the eulogy in there with him, and sat down. I felt cold and hot all at the same time.

The final blessing was emotional, and the smell of the burning incense is one I can still smell each time I close my eyes. As the final hymn began, everyone descended on us again—holding us, offering condolences and all I wanted was to hold Dada one last time.

The pallbearers lifted the coffin, and I saw them taking him out. I ran after them. This couldn't be my last goodbye. By the time I reached them, they had already placed him in the hearse and covered his face with a starched white handkerchief. I screamed, "Wait!" and told them that I wanted to say goodbye. I climbed in, kissed him multiple times, tears streaming down my face, my heart breaking over and over again. I tore myself away and stood aside watching them cover his face again and then bringing in the lid of the coffin. Then the lid shut, closing in a life that was lived gregariously and putting a physical door between me and my dad.

I can't remember much after. The numbness isolated me from the reality before me. People were talking to me and telling me nice things about Dada and all I could really hear was the deafening sound of silence. It was like my auditory senses decided I've had enough.

Some people, who had recently lost their own parents, told me how the pain would never settle and I had to prepare for a lifetime of missing them. While they were saying these things I could not speak back, but in my mind I was screaming, *I know! Don't say it to me and make it more real than it already is.*

My Dada was not even in the ground yet, and still people around me were telling me things like, "Be strong, he would not want to see you cry." Or, "Don't cry, dear, your mom will feel worse." And of course, the line I still hate: "He's in a better place now."

Yeah, I know he's in a better place. I'm glad—but I am here and he is not, and that's an awful place for me.

People really should be taught how to speak to someone who's grieving. There should be some course on how to deal with bereaved people because this world is really insensitive and horribly illiterate on this. Sometimes I wonder why people think they have to say things. It would be much better to just give the person a hug or an arm squeeze and say nothing at all.

The burial was peaceful. The cemetery, as I said before, was peaceful and calm. The hole was way too shallow, I remember thinking. Prayers were said, people responded, and then the coffin was lowered into the ground. Even now, when I close my eyes, I can hear the sound of the mud hitting the coffin—a sound that will forever haunt both my waking hours and the nights I try to sleep.

After the burial, people once again came to offer their condolences. They said some sweet things about Dada and that was when I began understanding the true legacy he was leaving behind. A legacy of kindness and compassion. Those two words were constants on everyone's lips.

The day we said goodbye
Was one in my memory etched;
Every sound, every word,
Left me wrecked and my face drenched.

Saying goodbye happened so many times,
But in that church it was clear:
There will not be another time
I get to hold you or wipe your tears.

The finality that I felt
When they lowered you into the ground
Was complete and real—
Like the mud on your coffin sound.

The day seems like years ago,
A memory distant and gone;
But your presence I feel till this day,
Like you've been here through the dawn.

Time moves differently—
That's what people did say.
Now I know what they meant;
I've known it since that day.

Afterwards, a few friends stayed back. We went home, clinked our glasses, and celebrated the magnanimous entity we just said goodbye to. There was laughter, there were tears, and a whole lot of people raised their glasses to him, saying "cheers."

My body had had enough. I fell asleep a little after one in the morning. My friend stayed the night. I remember her lying at the edge of the bed, while I slept on the inside touching the wall. This was the first night I actually nodded off.

And then, I had the dream.

# CHAPTER 6

# THE DREAM

Ever since the day Dada passed, I started looking for signs that he was okay. I kept replaying thoughts in my head of all the days from the time he got sick. I was on edge; any thought, any memory, any situation would get the tears flowing. As I said earlier, guilt was one feeling I just couldn't shake.

Could I have done something more? Could I have made things better? Could I have saved him? Did I do enough?

That last question rang in my ears every day since he passed. *Did I do enough? Did he know I was there right through? Did he know I loved and cared for him? Did he know??????*

My mind was a whirlwind of thoughts, fighting an internal battle. A battle that had me tear through my insides in agony. I just needed to know if he was safe. There were so many questions about what happens after death, and nothing I read satisfied this curiosity or quieted the screaming within.

That night, the night we buried him, I went to bed, and that's when I got some sort of answer.

As I mentioned earlier, I was very aware of myself and how I was sleeping. Sometime after I drifted off to sleep I heard this gentle knock on my door and a distinct shuffling sound, like slippers shuffling against the floor of someone struggling to get their footing. I remember getting out of bed softly, trying not to wake my sleeping friend.

I opened the door. There was mom, clutching on to Dada's right arm. With a smile on her face and fear in her eyes, she said, "Look, look—your father has risen from the dead."

I said nothing but took in the sight in front of me. There stood Dada, eyes downcast, shirtless, in his blue Jockey shorts. He was shuffling his feet, trying to balance as mom struggled to hold him up. I took over, guiding him to the living room where I helped him into a chair facing the sofa.

From somewhere, a basin of water appears with a towel draped on the edge. I dipped the small hand towel into the water, squeezed the extra water out, and began wiping him down. To this day, when I close my eyes, I can still feel that motion.

I kept looking at him, flopped in the chair, unresponsive. As I kept wiping him, I heard his voice, strong and young. I looked up, and on the sofa opposite, there he sat, strong and smiling.

He looked how he did when we were both young, wearing a maroon pinstriped shirt he used to wear to work and his classic cream pants. He sat with his arm draped on the back of the sofa and his legs crossed.

I was still clutching tight to the Dada in the chair, while the one on the sofa smiled and said

"This feels good, this feels very good. I'm feeling very good."

As he spoke, I kept wiping the Dada in the chair and it became more difficult to feel his skin. I felt my hands only touched the air. I tried my best to hold on. I tried to hug him but I only felt thin air. I didn't want him to go but I could feel he was disappearing, as the one on the sofa looked more real and vivid.

He kept smiling. "I'm feeling good," he said again. "This feels great."

But I was still trying to hold on to the one that was fading in the chair.

I woke up with his voice still ringing in my ears—"I'm feeling good, this feels great." My face was drenched in a mixture of tears and sweat. I couldn't express in words what I had experienced so I just kept quiet. I was trying to make sense of all of it for myself. How could I speak to anyone else about it?

I went silent that morning. Was that just a dream? It felt so real.

I decided to confirm it with mom.

"Have you seen Dada's blue jockey shorts?" I asked mom later.

"That's what we put him in when he took his last journey out of this house," she said.

I was in total shock.

At breakfast, everyone was reminiscing about him. I couldn't eat or speak. I just stared in silence.

A message you sent me,
A sign from above;
I knew you were okay—
You shared that with love.

My troubled mind,
You tried to ease;
A short little visit
From a soul at peace.

You showed me you felt me
Look after you with love,
Until the day you slipped away—
Went home, like a dove.

And in me dreams you told me,
I'm never alone;
You are in my heart,
You are never really gone.

Eventually, I mustered the courage and told those at home about my vivid dream the previous night. Everyone looked at me with disbelieving eyes. I felt like it would have been better had I not opened my mouth and let that be my little secret with dad.

Some humoured me, nodding along to all that I was saying but I know they didn't believe it. I felt the stares that spoke a story of sympathy and pity but not so much belief in this other worldly experience I just had. I didn't try to get them to believe me because I knew how that dream felt. I knew how it had moved me, scared me, but also calmed me. It soothed my anxious mind and my restless heart.

It was then that the real mourning began. It was then that true grief kicked in and I started grieving the loss of my dear Dada. It was that dream that took me and the relationship we had out of the equation for a bit and allowed me to appreciate the last moments we shared.

From pressing his legs everyday after work, to joking with him about his "meal of tablets," to walking in with the insulin injection with an evil grin that he laughed at, right down to holding his hand through it all and not leaving his side for anything. That dream showed me that those memories we made meant everything to him. It solidified in my mind and in my heart that he was with me forever. Maybe I would not see him in his physical form anymore but he has created me, so the biggest part of him is forever lodged in the largest part of my heart.

Yes, this chapter may be the smallest in this book, but it's one of the most special to me. What am I even saying? It is all special, but this is the soothing of the heart that I so desperately needed.

# CHAPTER 7

# Grief Begins

From the 20th of November onwards, the real grief story began. Grief is not easy to describe. It is a very individual journey that you go on—one that knocks you into shape and yet unravels you at the seams. It is like a train journey. You can travel in an absolutely packed compartment. After all, many around us have lost loved ones, yet it is a very lonely journey because no passenger experiences it the same way. No one can say, "I know what you are going through," and actually mean it. Grief is a solo trip, one where it is just you and your memories, just your loved one and your relationship with that person and just you and your yearning for that person to be back in your life.

For those who do still resort to the "I know what you are feeling," please stop. Nothing will ever make that statement true. Human beings are complex, and each connection we make is so different from the other. Logically, it's a complete fallacy to even consider that we know how the other person is feeling. This holds for every human experience, but for grief it's a much louder, resounding: **"No—you don't know what I am feeling, so stop saying that."**

Goodwill is definitely what people mean but the way it comes across to a griever is very different. In this chapter, I will try to explain in words what I have found to be the most difficult to describe emotion I have ever felt.

Is grief a feeling? Is it an emotion? Or a reaction? I don't know the correct answer, because to me grief is so much more. It is like an entity unto itself—something that builds up inside you, demanding attention every minute of every day. In the first month or two, it is a parasite that latches on and won't let go. You try to shake it off but no! It just clings to everything you do or say. You're talking to someone, and out of nowhere you feel it well up in your throat and hear your voice quiver. I have always wondered if I was sensitive and emotional, as tears didn't easily flow before this experience. Now, tears are my constant companion. In the first few months, you actually feel this parasite ravage every vestige of normalcy you ever had. It rips you apart and leaves you in shreds by the side of the road.

As the first month came to a close, we had a very intimate and personal Mass in his memory. It was peaceful. Joanne and I decorated the grave as best as we could. Dada loved orchids, so we brought as many as we could and placed them lovingly on the earth that now held him in its grasp. The cross was finally placed on the grave to mark where he lay, and the dance of the orchids seemed quite rhythmic as we said a solemn prayer there. Birds sang their melodies in the tree above the site, oblivious to the pain enveloping us here down below. Again a dichotomy of joyful melody and heart-wrenching wails.

30 days to the day we put you here,
Buried beneath the earth;
30 days since we last saw your face,
And now memories do hurt.

The world continued its tango,
Up and down went the beats;
But home has been absent of laughter—
We are glum in our seats.

30 days doesn't seem like a lot
When everything is normal and fine;
But it seems like a decade of longing
When the earth has taken what's mine.

A solemn prayer by the grave site,
With the birds chirping above—
The air was full of longing,
And missing your unrelenting love.

In months one and two, time took on a completely new feel. Days were running by yet seemed to be taking forever. I couldn't wrap my head around the passage of time. That first week after, I panicked. I could feel that day slipping further away from me, and for some reason I just couldn't stand the thought of days from that last touch racing away from my grasp. I thought things would soon calm down in my mind and my heart. In that first month, I felt overwhelming guilt every time I smiled and laughed. There were many opportunities to smile as people who loved me and cared for me from everywhere around came to spend time with me. Feeling that love was heartwarming and overwhelming all at once. The weird thing about grieving is the emotional dichotomy: happy and sad, distraught and grateful, lost and loved... they all seemed to happen together.

Every picture I had of him in my phone I clung to with all I had. I wanted to collect every picture, even the ones with him in the background. I went through mom's phone and sent myself the pictures she had of him. I went through his phone and that was like opening Pandora's box. He loved nature and had photographed every bird and butterfly he could come across. But the first picture in his photo album stopped me in my tracks. It was a picture of me, taken when I was ordering some food on the last outing we took him on. On the way back from the doctor, he said he wanted some coffee, so we went to a new coffee shop that had tea cakes and coffees and he was elated! The doctor had just given him a strict diet, but I decided he's going to have what he wanted. So we had coffee and pastries and his smile was infectious that day. There was no sign of pain, just happiness. When I was completely unaware, he clicked a picture of me. That was the last picture he took.

Everything he touched was as it had been—like a photograph from which one major object just faded away. That was what home looked like now, an incomplete portrait. He loved to sing and would be singing all day, and now there was silence—louder and more disturbing than a thunderstorm on a dark scary night.

His chair still sits there, lonely and bare. Every morning he'd sit there with his papers, doing his crossword puzzles, one leg draped around the arm, his back resting against the other. Now that chair sits unused, vacant and sad, like it has lost its essence. When people visit, I still shudder when they choose his chair to sit on. His bedside table still holds the pieces of paper he would write on: Recipes from the various shows he would watch, a back scratcher that he'd wield around with a laugh and his glasses on the top of the stack. Everything is where it ought to be except him.

Holding on to all of these things became like an anchor. Society, however, frowns on any display of cherished clutching. I can't tell you how many people said, "You have to let him go, or he will never rest." There is so much people need to know about grief and how to handle a griever but alas, we humans only think that we know what is right and we know it all.

With time, you get used to this parasite called grief. You even begin holding on to it like a crutch. Soon, the whole feeling of it turns into a routine. It's always there, lurking in the background and when you least expect it, it hits you like a wave. Many describe grief as something that you experience in waves, and I agree whole heartedly. Sometimes, the sea is calm and the waves predictable. At other times, the sea is stormy and waves crash down on you like a ton of bricks. Most of the time, they are gentle and it is in those moments that you sometimes forget they are really not coming back.

There were plenty of days when I woke up on a holiday and thought "I wonder if **they're** awake" and once I opened the door, realised that it is not **them** anymore. There are still times when I have been in another room and have heard talking and thought nothing of it because in my head, "it's just mom and Dad talking," and after a few minutes it dawns on me. There are times I'll be sitting in the living room and see a slight movement out of the corner of my eye and think absolutely nothing about it because hey, "that's probably Dada pottering around again." I still experience this, more than ten months down the line. So it gets me thinking, can 74 years of existence just completely cease to exist?

You are never really gone
Your legacy exists still;
You might not be here in body,
But in heart you always will.

The journey you have travelled,
With your laughter and your smile,
Has not been erased completely—
It will be here a long while.

And while there is a huge absence,
Sounds, sights and feels don't hide
That you will be ever present—
An Angelic, witty new guide.

When Dada was here and I knew we were losing him, I thought, *okay, grief is at my door.* I never really understood how consuming this thing called grief would be. The moment he took his last breath is when it entered. I felt it in every fibre of my being—like each cell went through a sudden significant transformation that could never be rectified or go back to normal. At that last breath I felt it dawning on me, things will never be the same again. Life as I've always known it has ceased to exist and a new normal was now about to be unleashed.

During this time, someone once said to me, "Losing a child is like losing your future, losing your partner is like losing your present and losing a parent is like losing your past." As she said it I knew I would not really understand all forms of loss until I lived it and I am going through the motions. With Dada slipping away, all I knew of my life slipped away too. Forty years of life had him in it. All my milestones thus far had his presence. From now on, he won't be there. That thought was daunting.

With everything that happened after the 17th of November 2024, I could only think of one thing: the last time this happened, he was here.

That first Christmas and New Year without him were sucker punches that just kept coming—just a month since he was gone. I know I dreaded it. Carols felt like stabs to the heart and Christmas wishes like kicks to the gut. "Merry Christmas to you and your family" and the smile would fade, the heart would pound. My family is now incomplete. I didn't know how to reciprocate the sentiment, especially because Christmas and New Year were his favourite times of the year, followed closely by Easter.

Memories crept in. Our last Christmas together was picture-perfect—laughter and so much joy. This one was so solemn; all we tried to do was get through the day. The words "Happy New Year" felt like a dishonour to his memory. How could this year be a happy one when we were leaving him back in the previous? That was a battle of gigantic proportions as I just couldn't get past the fact that he was not coming with us into 2025.

It is these thoughts that drove me insane in the early days after Dada's passing. The thoughts of: *Did it hurt? Was he in pain at that last moment? Did I do enough? Could I have saved him?* My goodness, how the mind takes you for a complete ride! Every thought, every action is somehow tied to the one you are missing and that in itself is a huge burden to bear. There were times wherein I'd feel all emotions at various times of that day, but then there were those days when I'd feel so many different emotions, all at the same time. Most of the time, I felt like I was losing my mind.

There were days when the mind would totally fail. I've always thought of myself as a very structured, calm thinker. Grief changed that completely. There were days when whole memories escaped retrieval and I'd be sitting there, in a battle with myself to make sense of what was going on around me. Grief is like a stealthy thief that robs you of tiny bits of yourself and who you formerly were, so slowly that you barely notice.

One day you're eloquent and can hold a conversation with absolutely anyone, and the next, you're scrambling for words in front of a class you've been teaching for five years. One day you're feisty and can stand up against any form of injustice and the next, you have no desire to engage with anyone, let alone stand up to fight for a cause. There were days when my mind would take a break and forget to tell me about it. I'd be sitting there ready for work and the mind just decided, *"ummm no thanks"*. I call it "grief fog"—the brain fog that suddenly decided to accompany me. Maybe that's how the mind copes: it shuts down.

With emotions so strong, there has to be some sort of coping. Maybe the body does these things to help you along and to prevent a sudden and complete short circuit of the brain and body. Never before have my emotions been so intense and so all-consuming.

The grieving mind is a different thing,
It shuts down when you least expect;
It does whatever it thinks is best,
But it leaves your life quite wrecked.

Moments of clarity are suddenly felt,
They come on in sharp bursts;
But then they disappear almost as sudden,
And that, then, is what hurts.

You are not the same anymore;
No, things have certainly changed—
Your mind that was once your friend
Is now a foe, and very deranged.

The grieving mind is a complex thing;
It needs a lot of deep study.
Is this something that will cure itself,
Or is it a life long worry?

Maybe I haven't read enough about grief. I don't know if there is much literature out there about all this, but these experiences are quite unnerving. It's one of the many reasons why I am writing this book. Maybe someone out there can take solace in the fact that this is not an isolated experience and we are not alone. Perhaps the griever's mind does exist—maybe it is the human mind's way of dealing with a flood of emotions that overload the system, shutting down parts in self-preservation. Well, I hope this is what it is and I hope it is something that passes. If I have learnt one thing in these last few months, it's that nothing stays the same. At first, that thought was also unnerving, but eventually it became something of a solace. Just the understanding that everything changes made it easy to tell myself that these intense feelings will eventually evolve into an easier, more bearable way of life. (More on this in a later chapter.)

The idea of loss transformed as the finality of this one hit differently. No prior loss was quite like this one. Just the idea of never seeing that face again or hearing that voice or even holding that hand was a thought too difficult to bear. How could this be so final? How could this be the end? Last year at this time he was absolutely fine. There was no indication that we would be in this space of utter shock and absolute loss.

This entire chapter may read like a complete confusion of emotions and ideas because the immediate aftermath was just that: a total and complete mix of emotions, thoughts, feelings and ideas—some of the major battles and the human flaws that we all display in relationships. I can't explain this clearly enough but I hope it does resonate.

In the immediate aftermath of death, those left behind go through a deep evaluation of life with the lost member. Every little slight and every small misstep first flies to the forefront of all memories. How could I have been so mean? How did I not see how important those moments were? How could I say such a thing? Why didn't I do more? Why didn't I save them? And the questions and self-criticisms go on and on and on. This was the hardest phase, and I don't think I am past it either. I still have those questions and those apprehensions.

The good news: there will come a time when the memories bring smiles, more often than the tears. Sometimes the very same memory will hurt and bring gratitude and happiness at a later time. One thing that I learnt in the first six months was that gratitude was the healer to the incurable wound. Every time I thought of the negative thoughts, I would say a soft "thank you" for the experience and the lessons I had learnt. Every time I beat myself up for not doing more, I said a little thank-you prayer for the peace with which he went. Every time I felt the unbearable pangs of his absence, I mumbled a thanks for the forty years I had with him.

That learning made it easier to breathe. Two small, simple, unassuming words: Thank you

"Thank you" is more than words together—
It is a feeling that heals the heart;
Thank you is more that a passing phrase,
It unites hearts rudely torn apart.

For the times we have shared and the memories—
I thank you so very much;
For all the love you have showered me with,
For the hugs and the soft gentle touch.

My world was a bright shining portrait,
Until the day that you left;
But I thank you for the deep lessons you taught,
Even though now we are left bereft.

I thank you for the moments of comfort,
For clarity when I needed advice;
I thank you for the strength you instilled in me,
For making me approachable and wise.

I stand today broken and teary—
But I know that all this will pass;
I thank you Dada for all that you have instilled in me
From you, all my strength I've amassed.

As we say goodbye to the ones we love, a few lessons I've learned are: **hold tight** to the love and the beautiful memories. Also hold on to the things they held dear. I still wear his watch along with my own—people think that I must have a lot of time on my hands (pun intended). **Do what they did** because that is keeping their legacy alive. I take pride in tending to his plants and now helping out in small ways like he did. Don't listen to the old tales of "don't keep going to the cemetery, they won't rest in peace." **Do what makes you feel good**—makes you feel close to them. **Speak to them** as if they are around, chuckle at the funny things they did and laugh—**oh my God, laugh!** It's a tribute to them, the lovely people they once were. **Talk about them;** keep their name on your lips. **Forgive** them and yourself, for we are all humans and have made and will make mistakes . But most of all, **be grateful** to them and for them. These are lives worth being grateful for.

Cherish memories and live to honour them... Always and forever more.

# CHAPTER 8

# SIGNS FROM ABOVE

This chapter is sure to get our sceptics' tongues wagging and their concerns for my mental health heightened. But it is what kept me anchored to the ground I walk on. So, for the sceptics, bear with me for a while.

Dada's photo gallery on his phone was full of pictures of nature, interspersed with a few very funny selfies he took of himself. Even before I opened his gallery for the first time, something strange started occurring around me.

The day after he passed, when it was just mom and me at home—me roaming aimlessly from room to room, looking for something to occupy my mind—was when I first experienced it. No—it wasn't something supernatural; in fact, it was something completely natural. I was standing at my window, which looks out over a valley. I remembered Dada standing there once and saying, "Such a beautiful, green space and yet, not many butterflies, huh?" And as that memory flashed, a big, white butterfly with yellow dots flew past my window. My heart raced and my head went into its general logical stance of "Coincidence, you psycho." But I couldn't shake that experience and said absolutely nothing about it.

Again, on my aimless roaming from room to room, I walked past the kitchen window, below which was a black platform. Dada would perch himself on that platform and eat his meals. I would always grumble at him for this distasteful habit and point him to the dining table. He'd always smirk at me, saying, "This is the most comfortable dining spot in the house." As I ran my hand over that platform and looked up and out of the window, another butterfly flew past at that very moment. This one had a darker hue and a slower gait. It fluttered around for ages and I stood there transfixed. This tiny creature, with its magical little movements, had stopped the tears that were involuntarily flowing since the previous day.

It could be nothing more than a coincidence, I kept telling myself. But from that day onwards, I'd rush to the window every morning hoping to see a butterfly or a moth or some winged creature. Lo and behold, there was never a lack.

The flutter of tiny wings,
Perched on the trees nearby
Were signs that I chose to hold
As signs of you from the sky.

The colourful grace that I saw
Sure reminded me of your face—
The joyful laughter and the smile
And the gentle movement with grace.

I checked your phone that evening
And what was the photo I saw?
Pictures and pictures of butterflies,
And a lonely little bird claw.

Was this your way of telling me
That you will always be around me with love?
Will you appear as a butterfly,
Or answer my calls with a dove?

Days that went by in a blur were interspersed with sharp signs that I never expected. I had never seen so many winged creatures before. There were moths as big as my foot (I have small feet, but they were still big) in my room on random days and, on one day—exactly a week after he passed—a white moth with black markings flew into my mom's room and perched there for two days. Finally, we found it dead on Dada's pillow. I know there will be plenty of sceptics calling it all coincidence. I was one myself, but the number of them was something I didn't anticipate. After the one-month service, mom, a friend and I went into town for lunch. On the way to the restaurant, we counted sixty-four bright butterflies flying past the windshield. I stopped counting on the way back.

It wasn't just butterflies either. There were birds too—not all birds, but specific ones that somehow found their way around us: peacocks, bulbuls and, my favourite, black drongos. These three have since been constant companions for us. Black drongos seem to follow me around and mom always sees bulbuls and peacocks. When I started this chapter, I spoke about Dada's gallery on his phone. Any guesses who his muses were? Correct; all these little winged creatures I just mentioned.

Some mornings I hear shrill sounds from the branch outside my window and, as I look out, I see drongos bringing the house down with their loud cries. The moment I look out, they shut up, almost smirk at me, and fly away. Yes, again, I know, this could all be coincidence, but for me now, this is comfort. This is how my pain takes a break each day. It's the moment in the day where I forget he's not around and, in fact, feel that he is still here, smirking at me and somehow conveying that he will always be around to guide and protect me.

In December, our beautiful state of Goa was abuzz with a very sacred event that occurs once every ten years. The relics of our patron saint, Saint Francis Xavier, are brought down for an exposition, where faithful followers come from far and near to venerate the sacred relics. We are blessed to be staying a stone's throw from the cathedral. Dada was excited about it but sadly didn't get the chance to participate. One day, mom and I were walking towards the cathedral for Mass. I was walking a few paces behind her and, at one point, something told me to look up. Like a masterpiece in the sky hung the most pristine rainbow—all seven colours distinct. There was no rain at all that day, no sign of any weather change; no one even noticed the beautiful semicircle above them. I pulled out my phone and filmed mom walking under it, completely oblivious to the magnificence above her. It looked like she was walking towards an embrace that he was sending from above.

After Dada passed, my awareness for nature grew more intense than ever before. In the first month, I heard the hoot of an owl outside my window. Over this year, that sound receded into the darkness again. As I was editing this book, I sat at my work desk reading through tears. As I kept reading, I heard a mild hoot. The hoot grew louder until I could no longer ignore it. It was as if an owl was sitting just outside my window. I stood to take a break, walked to the window and looked out at the pitch-dark outlines I could make out. I asked Dada, "Why do I only hear the owls? Why don't I ever see them?" This happened on a Wednesday.

The same Sunday, after Mass, we went to the cemetery, as we do each Sunday. I looked at a tree a few metres away, diagonally to the left of where he lay. Right there, perched on the tree, was a little baby owl. Bright sunshine all around and this little cutie hopped a bit, looked about, hung around long enough for all of us to get a good look, and then hopped out of the frame. Dada probably said, "I always give you what you want, don't I?"

Another strange experience that I often have now is this strange popping in my ear. I could be sitting around doing absolutely nothing and a slight change in my auditory sensation is felt, like a puff of air gently blown into my ear. Non-threatening, not at all irritating—just a slight enough change to experience the sensation. At first I thought my ears needed to be checked or cleaned out. So I did all that, but the sensation would still return every now and then. It was like a tiny whisper of "hey there". I smile every time I experience it, as in my heart, I believe that Dada pops in, on and off, to just check in.

There are times when I will catch a shadow out of the corner of my eye. At first I ignored it as "just Dada pottering around". Then it would dawn on me—he isn't here to potter around anymore. I would also hear the sound of him moving around, and I guess that's why the confusion. Maybe it's just my mind being so used to him that it would replay memories of the only world I knew. Maybe it's my brain trying to compensate for the sudden disappearance of this central character in our home. Or maybe, just maybe, it is a little sign from a world I cannot see, reminding me that his soul and spirit remain as my guardians, even though the body has ceased to exist.

On the 26th of September 2025, Dada's first birthday in heaven, I signed up with my publisher. I was uneasy all morning and decided to come home early from work. I stood at my window and said, "Happy Birthday, Dada. I signed up with a publisher and that is your birthday gift. Hope you like it." In hope of receiving a sign, I asked for something I thought would be impossible. Earlier, I mentioned the black drongos. Since the beginning of the monsoon season, I had only seen maybe one drongo. I was missing them tremendously. So I asked Dada to send me one if he liked my gift. I stood there for ages, but none came. I gave up hope and got around to doing my work again. In the evening we went to the cemetery to lay a bunch of flowers at his grave. As soon as I got out of the car, there, perched on the tree in front of the cemetery, was a beautiful black drongo. It swooped around twice, made its presence felt long enough for me to show mom, and then disappeared. I had my sign from Dada. He loved my birthday gift to him.

The tiny things that remind me
Have now become my comfort;
They are what I hold on to
Whenever pain I confront.

People look at me weirdly
When I explain the little feelings,
But no one will get the comfort
Until confronting the same dealings.

The signs from above I hold to,
Not caring how they judge—
To those who grieve I tell you
Stick to your own beliefs, don't budge.

For grief is more than can be explained;
It needs patience to comprehend,
So let your thoughts free to change—
Let your belief systems bend.

The smallest signs became my anchor. Me—a sceptic of all things supernatural—was experiencing a quantum shift. I did have a choice to begin with: bury my feelings and move on, or evaluate them, feel them, explore them and then move forward with them. I chose the latter, and I am glad. In all our years together we had not spent more than two weeks apart and now, even though we are in different realms, I've never felt closer to him. All thanks to my little signs and a lot of blocking out of society's indoctrination of how one should grieve.

The world called all this coincidence, but for me, it was solace and signs that he would forever be around, watching and guiding me as I lived the rest of life missing him.

They never really go far away—this is what I learnt. They only go as far as you let them. If you hold on to things that are special to the both of you, you hold them for an eternity. What better way to honour the ones whose lives shaped your own other than welcoming the signs they are sending you, and smiling the smiles that lit up their worlds when they were here and even after they have transcended?

# CHAPTER 9

# Every person has a role to play

This phase showed me the best and worst of people. What I lost this year went beyond Dada. I lost more than half of myself, and I chose to let go of another huge chunk of people who would flit in and out of my life. What I realised about grief is that it takes away the patience to deal with those who do not align with you. Probably they never did, but grief pulls away that veil that was drawn over your eyes. I realised that we have those who are:

- There for the good times
- There for what you can do for them
- There for what they can do for you
- There for the bad times
- There for every type of time

Times like these show you who you can't count on: the ones who essentially forget you exist but appear at the funeral; the ones who knew he was in the hospital but chose to wait till he was gone. When you lose someone, you realise—with clarity—who you need around you and who to just cut off.

In those days when he was ailing was when I needed people to just pat me on the back and tell me that I could do it. And yes, there were loads. However, when he was in the casket, people came to me saying, "If there is anything you need, just give me a call." No thank you. Now I just need to be with the people who truly care for me.

When you lose someone, their life starts turning into a sort of a movie that replays constantly. You find yourself remembering people you haven't thought of in ages. You remember how it's been years since a particular person came over for a drink or dinner. You wonder where they are now. Then it dawns on you: they stopped turning up when the party stopped (metaphorically). They found other places to find their fun. **The "there for the good times"** people only hang around for as long as the going is good.

When the party was on,
And the music played,
You hung around,
And around him stayed.

The moment the good times
Ceased to exist,
You walked away slyly—
You made your exit.

There are plenty like this;
They are wherever you are.
The moment there's bad times,
They are curious from afar.

They hide behind excuses—
"I was busy last week."
But now I see clearly:
Comfort with you, I'll never seek.

My Dada was a well-known guy. When he was in his prime, his phone would constantly ring. He was the one people called if they wanted to have a gala time and—oh!—how he delivered. When he retired, only the true ones hung around. There were those who would suddenly flood his phone with pleasantries and then ask the question that was intended: "Can I borrow some cash?" or "I'm going on a holiday—do you have contacts to help with my stay?" And he would always follow through, for some reason. Loans were always given, calls were always made—for that was the kind of person he was. No expectations, just help. Very seldom were the favours returned, but that didn't matter to him, for he never found himself needing the favour in the first place. These people here were the **"there for what you can do for them"** people—the ones who embrace you when they need you and forget you when they don't. Sometimes the **"there for the good times" lot** are also the **"there for what you can do for them" lot**.

So many lives on the journey you crossed,
So many lives you touched and were engrossed.
Many a time, they were there for a hand-out
But when you ailed, they stood far away and out.

"Can I have a few thousands? My kid's getting married."
"A little late on payments, can you help me? I'm worried."
Not a blink of an eye, requests never denied;
"I'll pay you back in double, oh! How they lied."

Still, with a smile, ever willing to help;
But those with hands stretched only took, so well.
No matter—now it's over, but his legacy remains:
Give without expectation, it's now you at the reins.

Sure, there are those who run helter-skelter to be by your side when the, as they say, "shit hits the fan". When everyone is running around and definitely going to be there, they will also come. For some reason, I saw quite a few of those: the ones who came the moment they heard of his passing and then went missing when the crowd faded. I appreciate these as well, but it sometimes is just not required. Sometimes, the family just needs all the space they can get without the added burden of having to go through the pleasantries of social interaction. Sometimes, just sending a text will suffice and that will mean more. Over the year after, I revisited those messages of comfort over and over again, and those felt like healing. To the **"there for the bad times"**: don't feel obliged. You don't have to. Just send in a text and leave it at that.

Of course, what you do does always come back, and Dada did a whole lot of good for a whole lot of people. With hearts swelling with gratitude we found people who just took over. While our whole world shattered, there were people who came in, let us take the load off our feet, and just did the heavy lifting. Mom's friends came and stayed with us through the first week; we had friends who helped with arrangements and got things done. We had family that came by and just sat with us as tears streamed down our faces. We had people from all over just calling up every week to check in. No expectations, just pure, genuine concern.

There were those who would call up, finish off with the pleasantries and then just stay silent while we spoke our hearts out about the person who was, is, and always will be. To those, I thank you with all my heart, as something we found difficult to find, was someone to just let us speak his name, over and over again. We found solace in the **"there for what they can do for you"** people. We had plenty. When things got bearable, they would slowly retreat, not wanting to intrude.

From the bottom of my heart, I thank you—
The ones who just stood by.
From the depths of my soul I'm grateful
For you just held me and let me cry.

No advice you tried to give me,
Just a gentle nod when I spoke.
The silence was all I needed,
As on my tears I would choke.

The world needs more like you—
The silent warriors in strife.
As a family broken by pain,
We thank you for being in our life.

You truly, from your soul, begin to realise who your people are: the ones that just don't let go even when you are kicking and screaming for them to leave you alone. I must say, I am lucky to be surrounded by those heroes. During the entire year, before and after, there were those who checked in and continued to check in. These were the ones who wanted your grief to just be about you and your pain. The ones who in no way wanted to make it about them. These, I realised, were the ones who have known loss.

They somehow just understand when to say what, and when to just back off and let one be. I am grateful for those who stuck by when I was inconsolable as well as when I was calm and composed. For they just somehow knew and could see the storm raging behind my steady eyes. My people who were **there for my every phase of life**. Very often the, **"there for what they can do for you"** people are also the **"here for my every phase of life"** people.

When I said, "I don't need you—
And leave me alone,"
You stood there beside me
As I shook to the bone.

When I asked you to hold on,
To give me my space,
You stood at a distance
But kept with my pace.

When I whispered, "I need you,"
You dropped all and came;
You handled things I couldn't—
You kept me from going insane.

I thank you for staying by,
Even when it was tough.
I feel the compassion,
The support and the love.

Many people came to bid him farewell. The church was packed with the tears and sniffles, reminiscing and sorrow. If only he knew how much he meant to people while he was still here. As a griever, that becomes a very heavy question: Did he know how much he was loved? Did people express how special he was to them? For me, that's what I wanted him to know! He was loved, is loved, and forever will be loved by us and all whose paths he crossed.

Within that internal battle there were other elements from the outside that really became a force to be reckoned with in the immediate aftermath, and for months on end. It's the people—there are just too many. All those people then descend on you. Yes, there are a few you want around and I realised, I was craving having people who spoke about him around me. What I didn't realise was that the people who came to talk about him, also came to give their advice and pointers on how to deal with grief. Yes, a lot of people have lost their loved ones and I'm sure, at that time, they wanted to help and share tips that really helped them. The fact, however, is that no one will be able to tell you exactly how to deal with **your** grief. That was my hardest learning, **no two people will ever go through it quite the same**.

What people don't understand is that each person knows exactly how to heal their own pain and if they don't, they will find the professionals that will help them get through. Sometimes, it is important to let people find their own strategies. Some believe that therapy tells you exactly how to deal with emotions, but a good therapist will not tell you what to do and how to do it, they will listen and subtly guide you to find your own ways of healing and dealing.

In the meantime, there are things we can all do, or, better still, avoid doing, to help people cope. I have listed them down here as a cheat sheet for anyone who cares enough to help a griever in the process. Of course, this is what I would have liked, some may want it differently so first and foremost, evaluate the situation and see if these fit the situation and the individual:

1. **Don't use their grief as a lesson for yourself, or, if you do, don't say it to them.** There have been times since I lost Dada that people have come up to me and said that my experience has encouraged them to go ahead and find ways to do things better with the members of their families. I'm so glad for all of them who used my misfortune as a way to right their wrongs but in the depth of my grief, that was the last thing I wanted to hear. How was I supposed to be okay knowing that my pain saved someone their pain but I did not have that chance? Just knowing that the end of my relationship came quicker and before I made the necessary amendments was torturous.

2. **Never say you understand exactly how they feel.** Firstly, that will never be true. Understanding the complexity of a relationship you just lost is difficult if not completely impossible. In this journey of my own grief, I have had friends who have too lost their fathers after I lost mine, and not in even one of those circumstances have I felt "ah! Here! I understand what she/he is feeling".

When you lose someone close, you lose more than the human—you lose the memories you created, the love you shared, the arguments you had, the inside jokes, the habits you formed together, the rituals you created, the moments you shared, the moments you lost, the words you spoke to each other, the words you forgot to speak to each other, and if I continue, the book will never end. With so much that's transpired, do you really feel you would be able to empathise completely? The weird part is, I also got this line from people who had not lost a parent. So best not to pretend to know.

3. **Don't wait for the dust to settle.** There is this invisible timeline that society puts on grievers. "It's been a month already", "It's been a whole year!" "Oh goodness! Five years have passed and she's still talking about it." Yes, a whole lifetime can go by and guess what! I'll still be talking about him, missing and grieving for him. That's just how grief is. It might not be a central feature in life for the observer but the griever has just learnt how to mask up and move forward. The world is no more privy to the tears that fall at night or the pangs of pain that rip through the soul behind the soulful eyes masked by a smile. Grief does not have a timeline nor does it have an end date. I have learnt that grief shall remain with me forever, for he was my Dada for my entire life and will always be.

4. **Talk about the lost person and use their name when talking to a griever.** One of my biggest fears, though completely unfounded, has been that people will forget how awesome he was. Personally, every time someone spoke

about him or said his name, it felt like a warm hug. Even those who didn't know him personally would bring him up in conversations I wanted to continue having. There is this fear of bringing up the memories of someone who has passed. I did it myself and I'd always tell myself it was because I didn't want the griever to feel worse. In truth, you only know when you know.

5. **Don't make the grief of others, your grief.** I remember feeling trapped, head wanting to explode at the mere mention of the "Oh I also went through this". Some people seem to be in competition for everything, including whose pain is worse. When those types of conversations were had, I just physically shut down. I stepped back and said, "You go. You feel your pain is more, go ahead. Shout it from the roof tops." Everyone deals with grief differently. I shut down, while others make it known that their pain is loud. No matter how loud, pain is pain. Just because someone chooses to suffer it silently, doesn't mean their pain isn't as bad or their grief has ebbed off. It just means that they choose to hold their relationship sacred. Hold it private. Only allowing the world to see what it is they want the world to see.

6. **We will all feel grief and that is the worst reality I have been battling with.** Yes, it's happened now, but it will happen again. When you are going through the daily grind, as a griever, this thought is another constant. There is a real fear of another loss. Thoughts like, "I cannot do this again" keep seeping in like a thief arriving to steal your

peace. A late message, a missed call, a delayed arrival, a slight fever or a cold, or a broken bone, sends the griever down a spiral of familiarity and foreboding. Remember this, and be courteous of their pain. Send out a message of reassurance or text to say you will call back, go to the doctor if you are unwell, if nothing more than to ease their anxiety. You never know until you know, and when you do know, that's when there is much to be feared and reexamined.

7. **Think before you speak, and speak only when necessary.** I stood there between two people in conversation: one had lost her child to a freak accident about six months prior, the other with a healthy baby boy growing up in all that developmental splendour. The one with the kid still around flippantly says, "Oh, we are very careful with how we see to his safety." I could feel a rock plummet into the pit of my stomach. Maybe time made them forget that they were talking to someone who is still battling something no parent ever should. That's the problem though. The freedom of speech is very often a freedom to hurt. This should be thought of even beyond grief. None of us know what the other is battling. So if you aren't going to think before you say it, don't say anything at all. Not even months after I lost my Dada, I stood there in conversations about how they would do anything to save theirs. My heart would plummet. Did I do enough? If I did, why isn't he still here?

8. **Maybe sometimes, just let them grieve the way they want.** That's the crazy thing about being human. The complex way in which we experience things. There are

moments when we just want to have them with us and nothing anyone says or does can make us feel any different. Just let them feel. Just let them be. Just let them cry. Just let them grieve. Let them do it the way they want to. There is no real way, no right way, no wrong way. There is only their way. .

9. **Life does in fact move forward, right from the day of that last goodbye.** No one who ever dealt with grief knows exactly when the pain is going to subside or when it is going to transform, but it does transform. However, it never really goes away. The first few weeks and months are gut wrenching pain. Breathing is laboured and the eyes seldom dry. As time passes, there is transformation and that transformation is nothing but growth. Grief does not go away or become less, we just grow into and around it. Like a jar that keeps getting bigger to accommodate its contents. So if the tears don't spill in your presence and if they laugh and seem like they are back to "normal", don't be fooled. There is no going back to "normal", there's no such thing. They've just got better at living a life they were never prepared to live. They've just found safer spaces to grieve and different ways to do so, so that society cannot feel awkward anymore.

Grief has so many faces, so many facets and so many ways of showing up. There are times I think back to a memory and the flood gates open and other times when the same memory brings a smile to my face. It's just such a complex experience that there is no answer on how to deal with it.

One face is downright tragic—
It never lets you sleep;
It causes so much heartache,
It's the face that's consumed by grief.

There is the pretender in there,
The face that goes on with life;
The face that smiles and laughs out,
But feels it alone, like a knife.

There is the face that cries softly
And leaves you confused and alone;
It is the face that comes gently—
That face makes you silently moan.

And then there is the face that feels guilty,
The face that is always asking why;
The "what ifs?", the "I wish...", the "how comes?
Will haunt till the day that you die.

There's the face that is constantly confused—
Wakes up and then by reality's hit;
The face that can't remember names anymore,
But alone with the memories sits.

All these faces are simultaneous;
They come on when you least expect.
They visit like phantoms unannounced—
Your forever unwelcomed guest.

Alas, most of us are clueless about grief and really don't know how to respond to it. Nobody knows till you actually know, but with this bit of my experience, I hope to give at least a little bit of a nudge in the right direction.

As a counselling psychologist, I have been trained in bereavement counselling. And I learnt all the theory and finally I realised I was doing it all wrong. There is no "one size fits all", no major theory that will explain how to get through this perfectly. There should be solace in that fact. For, right here, now, I feel gratitude for how beautiful human relationships can be. It is this beauty itself that leads to grief.

Grief is love extended and transformed, and it is because I have loved deeply that I grieve deeply.

And so, grief just seems to be the price we pay for love.

# CHAPTER 10

# GRIEF AND THE BODY, GRIEF AND THE MIND

**His last breath was my first with a wounded soul.** It is difficult to explain but the feeling of pain from loss is a permanent tear in the fabric of your life—one that might be darned but will never ever be completely mended. It feels like your entire being suddenly shatters and you then spend the rest of your life trying to pull those fragments together. As these fragments disperse all over, your body and mind start feeling very different. At least, mine did.

## GRIEF AND THE BODY

My first evaluation is of **sleep and rest**. I was always a light sleeper and very aware of that, but I would still wake up rested. When Dada fell sick, my sleep got even lighter. I would wake up everyday at around 3:30 or 4:00 a.m. to check on him. I did this for about two months before he passed. After he passed as well, I would wake at the same time and, almost on autopilot, get out of bed to go check on him. I still wake up at that time but don't get out of bed anymore. I just say a silent prayer and go back to sleep.

Another thing about sleep after loss was the dreaming. For about four months after he passed I just had dreamless sleep. I remembered nothing and woke up exhausted. I believe this was because my mind was on overdrive. I did not wake up rested anymore. Instead, I woke up feeling like I had been hit by a bus—aching body, sore muscles and an anxious mind. At first I didn't see a connection between this and my grief, but slowly, as I started paying more attention to my body and reflecting on how I was before, it dawned on me that my sleep was being affected by my feelings post-grief.

So I took matters into my own hands and started meditating again. I also started journalling again, giving myself the opportunity to feel tiny bouts of gratitude for the smallest possible win. Soon enough, sleep became more restful and the mind less anxious. What I realised from this simple hack was that the more I pour out, the less there is to stagnate within. Some might use therapy as their catharsis too. In whatever way possible, let the feelings out. My catharsis was in writing this book.

Another thing that I felt after I lost Dada was **physical fatigue.** My body refused to respond to activity in the way it did before. To a point where I stopped trying completely. I didn't feel like going for that walk, nor did I want to engage in that activity. I just wanted to fuse and become one with the couch and not have to move until I completely and totally had to. That led to its own set of problems, all having to do with pain. The physical manifestation of emotional cessation.

Here, the only thing that helped was to do it anyway. I didn't want to go for a walk, so I walked anyway. I didn't want to use the hula hoop (My favourite form of exercise), so I used it anyway. If, while grieving, you wait to want to do things, you just won't get around to doing them. So just do it anyway. Physical fatigue is connected to the lack of activity and the lack of activity causes that fatigue—A whole vicious cycle you just don't want to get entangled in.

A few weeks before the 15th of August in the following year, my body started crumbling. The **pain** was undeniable. Every area of my body felt like it was breaking down. My jaw hurt, my knees felt like putty under my weight, my ankles screamed with every step, and my back felt like it was disintegrating under my skin. I didn't understand why or what was going on. I read up on things and watched videos (given my new avoidance of medical spaces) ,and a common thread popped out: Grief also has a physical reaction—pain—one that can't be ignored.

Here, physical healing is required as the body keeps a memory of the trauma it's been through. Why the 15th of August? Because the year I lost my dad, the 15th of August had a significance: it was the day things started going downhill and he was hospitalised for the first time. I don't know how to explain the physical pain, just that my body did feel ravaged by the strain last year; the year that followed seemed like a re-enactment of that pain for some reason—a re-enactment with absolutely no real physical cause. It is like a physical memory of what you experienced before coming back to remind you.

Another thing I realised about myself was the **eating**. In the first few weeks, I didn't eat nearly enough to sustain, and then food became my solace. I ate when I missed him, I ate when I was angry at him, I ate when my memories of him made me smile, I ate when my memories of him made me cry. Food has a tendency of creating a very toxic relationship between you and your emotions. (Oh well, it actually is the emotions that lead the food and self to create toxicity, but we all tend to place blame outside of ourselves.) What was the solution? Mindfulness.

Be mindful about what you do, say and of course... **eat**. This is relative to the person going through it, but in most of the discussions I've had, I've noticed this pattern crop up. How do you be mindful? Take a step back and stay in the moment of where you are. If food seems to be pulling you close, ask yourself if it's needed right now. If you have food in front of you, eat it with awareness. Put your devices down when you eat and be completely present to that process.

Our bodies try to cope,
They struggle from within;
They take our emotions
And try to deal with them.

They use every way possible
To cope with the cascade;
They fight with all their might
Till their complete strengths fade.

The body has a way
To deal with the pain—
It just completely messes with
The mind and the brain.

And so we go to point one,
We go back to the start:
Grief causes us to break down
And deal with a broken heart.

## GRIEF AND THE MIND

The mind is a completely different ball game. **The grief fog**, as I like to call it (and mentioned earlier in the book), comes and goes. Some days it is very distinct; on other days, it is a light difficulty in tasks that need focus. This started almost immediately for me. I would be in the middle of something and—bam! I have no idea what I'm doing and why. I sometimes feel it is the mind going into autopilot. So everything you do is happening automatically while the mind tries to hold on to everything. When I mean *everything*, I mean that in the first two months after I lost Dada, I just kept replaying the last week to the point where I could recall every moment, every sigh, every word spoken among the rest of us as he lay there waiting for the gentle whisper from the angel of death.

The fog got so intense at around the four-month mark that I really thought normal functioning was near impossible. How did I deal with it? I made lists—I make lists—and I think that is my new normal. I have notes everywhere: things to do, people to meet, things that were said. I've started writing everything down. It is tedious, but it is also gratifying to be able to check things off my to-do list without hitting my head at the end of each day saying, "Shit, I forgot again".

Another mental experience I have had is the constant thoughts of **fear of losing others**. Every time someone leaves home, I fear that they may not return. Every mild illness is comprehended as a debilitating disease that will turn terminal. On the exterior, I have been like a rock, but internally I'm a nervous wreck, waiting begrudgingly for the next tower to fall. After you lose someone so close, the fear becomes very real. Almost like a foreboding. Even though is it completely unfounded. The fear of losing again, for me has been manyfold:

- I don't want to feel grief so harshly again
- I can't survive another time like this
- Will another grief experience take away from the grieving I'm currently doing? (And it is this one that I am, at this moment, very aware of.)

I do not want his memory to be marred by anything. If someone tries to contradict even a small fact in what my mind has created, I go into **immediate defensive mode**. My mind has created a narrative about his final year and if anyone remembers a moment of it differently, it unnerves me. I panic: "What if my entire recollection was wrong?", "What if he didn't know I really loved him?", "What if his final days weren't as peaceful as I remember them to be?" If I could get one fact wrong, I could have got them all mixed up right?

Another thing I've noticed is my constant **irritability**. I have been irritable with almost everything and almost everyone, almost all the time. I've noticed irritability towards people who boast about their plans with their dads; irritability towards people talking about their dads, both living and deceased. I have been quick to temper, for my threshold of dealing with nonsense decreased exponentially. My mind and heart have no place for small talk and frivolous banter. Keeping the peace is all I have been striving to do, so dealing with my irritability was indeed a very lonely and stifling journey. Pre-grief, I would just go with the flow, post-grief, my mind doesn't comprehend the need for people and situations that sap my already shaky emotional balance. So, I walk away from drama and keep myself rooted in things that bring me peace—moments in nature, getting lost in the pages of books, or journalling away the irritability and surrounding myself with people who are good for my emotions.

And that leads me to the contradiction to the above: **numbness**. Even though I have been experiencing a whole array of emotions, the feeling of numbness has been seeping into practically every one of them. It is so difficult to describe in words, but it has been such a conundrum that I am still trying to figure it out myself. It's like, I know I am angry, I feel angry, but my deeper feeling is numbness. A reaction of "Whatever" to something that would usually insight more emotion. Every feeling is laced with a numbness I never ever knew, but I fear it is a numbness that is here to stay.

Usually, time with friends would really be my escape and something I really looked forward to. In the days and months that followed, **social isolation** became my space of solace. I looked forward to alone time—time I didn't have to be focused on conversation and connection. I just wanted to be in my own company, aloof, forgotten by the social circles I travelled through all my life. I cringed when my phone rang and would watch it ring till it stopped; I allowed notifications to pile up, not even with the slightest curiosity of what messages they might hold. I basked in spaces that were empty and gasped for air in those that held even one other presence. The need to disappear gnawed at me feverishly. It took ages for me to accept an invitation to go out for a meal. In the early days, leaving home was riddled with guilt. I felt like I was leaving him and going out. Eventually, I relented and the first outing was difficult, but like everything else, it slowly got lighter and felt better. I still prefer spending a day with my thoughts and memories, but now the outside isn't as daunting. All it really took was that first time...

So much of my life has now turned into the **fear of forgetting**. Every day when I wake up, the first thing I do is run through a checklist. I think about his face, I try to recall his voice, especially how he would call out to me, how his voice danced with laughter and reverberated when he sang. I think about how his perfume smelt and how he would splash it into his hands and then dab it on his cheeks. I think about his smile and how his eyes crinkled, how he held up the newspaper every morning and sipped his tea. I think about how he walked and how he sat and only after I have gone down the entire checklist do I get out of bed. Every time I pass his pictures on our walls

I look at them intently, making sure each image is burnt into my brain for later retrieval. Every time his name comes up in conversation, even if it is someone narrating a dream they had about him, I listen intently and ensure that it goes into long-term memory. I look at his handwriting and at the things he left behind and promise myself often that I will not forget. I can never forget.

When I hear about the illnesses of old age and how sometimes the memory fades, my first fear is that I don't want to lose my memory of him.

The very essence of how I used to think
Will never be what it was;
The very foundation of how things were
Has a much deeper feel and cause.

It's like I woke up one day—
I really woke from slumber;
For all my life I lived on the surface,
And now I live from under.

A veil of something has been lifted,
And now I clearly see:
The so called life we are all living
Is much larger than you and me.

There is lots hidden from plain sight—
There's mystery and lots of intrigue.
Who thought losing part of your heart
Would introduce you to the bigger league?

Grief changes the very constitution of what made you who you are and were. People who have not lost will think there is an end date to grief. This is because people who have lost start living again. They go back to the humdrum of life and, on the outside, everything has gone back to what it was. On the inside, however, there will never be a going back. It is like this from now on out. Your whole world changes; the way you see the world changes and the way you perceive every other thing, changes. You move forward—you don't move on.

# CHAPTER 11

# AND SO… LIFE GOES ON

And so… life goes on… or does it?

As I said at the end of the last chapter, we never really move on. All we can do is move forward. How can anyone really move on from so much of your life? The memories we made, the traditions we created, the conversations we had, the experiences we shared—altogether they created a life we lived. That life being a beautiful tapestry of moments. Why would anyone ever want to move on from there? My life hasn't really gone on. For me, the day he took his last breath, life transformed into something different. Something deep, something more profound. Living life is not a reckless acceptance of what is anymore; it has turned into a life in memorial of him.

Losing a parent is like losing such a large part of your past—such a large chunk of your identity. When someone says, "Oh! You are Clarence Farrell's daughter," something inside me stirs. It was a sentence I grew up hearing, but now, there is a change. It is heard with a tinge of nostalgia, where earlier it was heard with pride, I still feel the pride but now there is the hint of sadness. I remember once, Dada telling mom, "When they were kids people would refer to them as my children, and now the world knows me as their father." The pride I heard in his voice still resounds, and I am glad for that memory. Now, I take each memory forward with me.

I now take interest in things he did and actually have begun seeing meaning in it. Something as wholesome as looking after plants was never something I cared enough for. I would look at the pots he lovingly placed on my windowsill as a barricade from the outside world. Now, it is my space of calm and my solace. In the days that followed his passing, I looked out of the window and happened to see his plants slightly wilting. At that moment, I took it upon myself to ensure their survival. In those first desperate days of knowing nothing about how to keep a plant alive, I struggled with the times of the day to pull out the watering can, the quantity that would suffice, and so much more. Slowly, as they started blooming under my care, a wave of peace washed over me—a feeling that whispered that he was proud of me. A feeling I want more of, constantly. So all he did suddenly had to be kept alive.

He took pride in his clothes and I? I would not even know what I had in my closet. Now, I make it a point to put in a tad bit more effort. I look for colours and styles that are more than the norm. I also iron my clothes with the passion he put in. I remember telling a friend years ago, "I don't know what to think. My Dada always ironed my clothes for school and now, he's still ironing my clothes for school (I am a teacher after all)." Every evening he would tend to each crease like it was a demon that needed immediate vanquishing. We would always squabble about what a shoddy job I would do with my ironing. Now, I iron with the same passion he taught me. When I am done, I hold up the cloth and inspect it like he did, and I grin at how well I got all those nasty creases, like he would.

Another area I would never dabble in was the kitchen. Dada loved to cook, and he did it with so much love. If he decided to make something, he would first ensure that every ingredient was perfectly chosen and placed on the counter, waiting for the absolute right time for him to swoop in there and work his magic. For me, cooking was a colossal waste of time. He always liked my cooking and would compliment what I churned out on those rare occasions that I dabbled—begrudgingly, I might add—but having the master chef himself in the room gave me a brilliant excuse not to bother. Now that he isn't here, from absolutely nowhere at all, I've developed quite an interest in this hobby of his. He would definitely be proud of the dosas I'm able to make and the various other stuff I've been experimenting with.

Everything you loved
Is now what I want to do;
It keeps me happy
And holds me closer to you.

Things that you loved,
I see the reason now;
I wish I had shared these
When you were here, somehow.

But in your memory
I will make it a point
To keep your hobbies present—
I will try not to disappoint.

Your passion was so complete
For everything you did.
I promise you, Dada,
I'll never keep those things hid.

What I am trying to say is this: life has suddenly turned into a memorial of him. Everything I do, everything I feel, moments when I have to make choices, are all dedicated to his memory. I ask myself very often, "What would Dada have done?" And in that moment I somehow know the direction in which I want to go. It is odd, this feeling, but it keeps me connected. It's like a telepathic conversation that we have. Even if it is only me making the decision, I will always be a part of him, so I like to think that the part of me making that choice is the part I inherited from him.

It is funny, and ironic, how things I clashed with him on have now begun to make more sense. Earlier, just because we differed on a viewpoint, I never took the opportunity to delve deeper and probably evaluate the situation from his perspective. Now, I try to get out of my own headspace and look at it from where he would probably be coming from. How I wish I had the courage and the ability to silence my ego and just look at things differently then. Those are some of the regrets I will always have. Not being able to just listen and think from his perspective. I now hold his values even dearer than I did when he was around.

When you lose someone, there is a shift. Once the initial shock ebbs off, you begin seeing the void they left and, if you can, you start trying to make that void less painful by keeping parts of them alive. Speak about them often. Bring up their name in conversation. I know people get uncomfortable speaking about those who have passed, but for those left behind, and in memory of the departed, it is important to keep talking about them. Their lives were too precious to be ignored and erased. The word *family* feels very alien now. Even when the rest of us go out, I find myself saying, "My mom, sister, niece and I went out." It is no longer "the family went out." Maybe with time it will be easier to say. But for me, family always meant us all with him.

**TO THE GRIEVER:**

Here are a few things for the grievers to ponder:

1. **It is okay to not be okay:** There is absolutely no compulsion to magically being fine. You have had a relationship with the person who is no longer around. No one will ever truly know the complexity of your relationship with the person and so there is no timeline for you to be okay. There will be days when you feel like the worst has passed, but then you will wake up and it will come crashing down again—and that is okay! There may be days when you just don't want to do things you normally did, or meet people and go on an outing, and that is okay too. You do not have to be

fine and pretend that you haven't just experienced an earth-shattering event, one that has changed the very essence of you.

2. **You can cry or not cry—that is your choice:** Not every person goes through grief the same way. I have heard so many people comment about how much a person is crying, or conversely, how little the person has cried. There is no correct amount of tears to be shed and no right amount of grief to be expressed. Whatever your heart feels and body responds to is perfectly fine. We need to normalise *not playing to the crowd.* When people are not around, only we know the pain with which we have to deal.

3. **The grief will come and go in waves and the waves will not cease.** I remember the day Dada passed—the feeling in my chest of absolute pain and hurt. That pain I thought would recede with time. I thought it would be a distant memory as time passed. On certain days, it does seem that way now. However, on more days than not, that pain comes back, overwhelmingly, to remind me of the word NEVER again. When I pass a photograph and see his smiling face, or when I get a whiff of a perfume that reminds me of him, or when I am just sitting around doing nothing and a thought of him crosses my mind, that pain returns brought on by the thought of "How can it be that I will never see his face or hear his voice ever again?" That pain is unlike anything I can truly explain. It is something that is physical but goes beyond—it is anguish that can be felt in your body and a silent scream that only you can hear.

4. **Grieving with another will be difficult:** Over the last few months, many people I know have also lost loved ones. Yes, empathising with another person's loss in the first few months after your own is not easy. Being able to express your condolences out loud will hurt. I felt overwhelmed and I just could not understand why. Then it dawned on me: the right words to say will never be completely right when dealing with loss. This experience is too profound for words to be enough. So all you need to do is lend an ear or extend a hug. If you can't find the words, that is fine. You don't have to say a word. A griever knows how another griever feels. You just don't have to say it. And yeah, again, don't try to empathise by saying, "I know how you feel." Let's normalise not having to say things like this too. For even if you have suffered the same loss, in my case, having lost a dad, no one will ever know exactly how *that* feels. Each relationship is way too personal for that.

5. **No matter the amount of time that has passed, the pain will not go away:** But it transforms—from heart-aching, fist-clenching, stomach-twisting pain to the dull weight of the void. Sure, people assume that with the passage of time, all is now good, and why won't they? We go back to doing things like we did before. It is a fact that we have to keep moving forward. The tears won't fall so easily and automatically as they did in the first few days and so, to the outside world, the wound may seem to have healed. The wounds, however, are still very much there—very much wide, gaping holes—but as time passes, we just grow into the role of dealing with it better. Externally, we seem put

together, but internally there has been a shift. I have spoken to numerous people who have lost loved ones—some a few months ago, for some, years have passed and for still others, decades have elapsed. Yet the pain lingers, the wounds remain, because the cost of deep love is finally, deep grief.

6. **Honour yourself and live life mindfully:** That is what they would want us to do. Smile more often, speak about them confidently and be unapologetically true to yourself. In these few months that have elapsed, I have learnt so much about so many things. Life teaches you about living, but death—it teaches you about life. For some reason, there are those out there who enjoy kicking you when you are down. These people see this as a chance to get that one-up which wouldn't be easy if you were at your best. However, what they don't understand is this: you have been through your worst ever experience. Absolutely anything they try to pull now pales in comparison to what you have been through. Also, you have an angel watching over you, so ha, looks like the joke's on them. Take pride in your smallest achievement. Even just showing up is such a profound feat, so honour yourself, be grateful for your tenacity and celebrate the small wins. For in a world that never stops spinning, you still manage to keep up.

7. **There will never be another them:** And that is actually a blessing. This society says we are replaceable, but in actuality, we are not. Just ask someone who has lost a loved one. No one will ever replace the love, the memories, the experiences and the space that a person has occupied in your life. We shouldn't hope to find them in another person and we shouldn't even try. The human experience is so beautiful.

We all have our parts to play and we all have the lives we are meant to touch. Each person that enters comes with their own special something, and we need to learn to appreciate all those little somethings. I have spoken to many who have lost children, partners, and friends. The response is always the same: there will never be another *them*, and that, my friends, is the ultimate beauty of life.

8. **The hardest part of grief is that time will not stop:** For me at least, the passage of time was a battle I did not anticipate. Time—it just keeps moving, and so does the world and all it holds. It moves, fast, loud, unrelenting, and yet all we want is to stop the clock. Dada passed in November of 2024, and as the new year rolled in I fought so hard to pull him into it with me, but I just couldn't. He remained in 2024 while all of us turned the page on the calendar. Every time I write the date, I'm reminded that he didn't see this year. Like that, I know there will be a number of years I will have to ring in without him. The knowledge of that hurts all over again. It seems like he's slipping through my fingers on the sands of time. So now, I have decided, I'm taking him with me and no one—and nothing—can do anything about it. I will do what he loved to do, I will continue his legacy and I will live for us both. That's how I learned I can cheat time and make sure it doesn't take from me what I want to hold on to.

A grieving heart hurts, it does;
The pain cannot be described.
There is a gaping hole in there
Where once love used to reside.

God took them back, on wings so bright,
Their work on earth complete;
But we are left with souls ripped apart
And in the corner an empty seat.

But all those years were not for nothing—
They left plenty when they went;
They were what got us through this life,
They, who heaven sent.

The lessons, words and memories
Form an album of their life—
One that holds steady, helps us move forward
And through them face all strife.

From what they taught us, what they shared,
We are much stronger now;
They gave us tools to fight it all—
We will get through somehow.

Knowing that we are taking their memory forward is the best balm for the pain. I'm sure there is nothing that they would want more than to see us take on life with the same gusto we always did when they were around. There will always be signs of their presence if you look for them and are willing to go beyond "reality" and just open your eyes and your heart. I hold on to the signs everyday. It is a ritual for me to look out of the window and spot those beautiful butterflies and think of his voice. I make it a point to say good morning and ask if he's doing okay and to say goodnight and hope he's had a great day. As I go about the house, doing the things he would do, I speak to him, clarifying if I am doing it right. Sometimes I get an answer; at other times I laugh and imagine him shaking his head in disbelief at my stupidity, like he would do. But I know most of all, he'd be standing there beaming with pride, happy that he taught me well.

There is so much left to learn about what lies beyond that veil that separates our two worlds, and in the months that have followed this loss, I have searched in books and videos and podcasts. But the truth is probably something we will only learn on that day when we close our eyes for the final time. And when that happens, I pray that I walk away, holding the hand that I lost that day, giving him an update on all he missed, and him smiling back at me, saying, "Hey, I was there for every bit of that journey, and I had a much better view".